THE MOST
TRUSTED NAME
IN TRAVEL

Frommer's®

Shortcut

SICILY

By Stephen Brewer
and Donald Strachan

FrommerMedia LLC

Published by
Frommer Media LLC

Copyright © 2016 by Frommer Media LLC. All rights reserved. No part of this publication may be reproduced, stored in a retrieval system, or transmitted in any form or by any means, electronic, mechanical, photocopying, recording, scanning or otherwise, except as permitted under Sections 107 or 108 of the 1976 United States Copyright Act, without the prior written permission of the Publisher. Requests to the Publisher for permission should be addressed to Support@FrommerMedia.com.

Frommer's is a registered trademark of Arthur Frommer. Frommer Media LLC is not associated with any product or vendor mentioned in this book.

ISBN 978-1-62887-230-9 (paper), 978-1-62887-231-6 (e-book)
Editorial Director: Pauline Frommer
Editor: Holly Hughes
Production Editor: Lindsay Conner
Cartographer: Liz Puhl
Photo Editor: Dana Davis and Meghan Lamb

For information on our other products or services, see www.frommers.com.
Frommer Media LLC also publishes its books in a variety of electronic formats. Some content that appears in print may not be available in electronic formats.

Manufactured in China

5 4 3 2 1

HOW TO CONTACT US

In researching this book, we discovered many wonderful places—hotels, restaurants, shops, and more. We're sure you'll find others. Please tell us about them, so we can share the information with your fellow travelers in upcoming editions. If you were disappointed with a recommendation, we'd love to know that, too. Please write to: Support@FrommerMedia.com

FROMMER'S STAR RATINGS SYSTEM

Every hotel, restaurant and attraction listed in this guide has been ranked for quality and value. Here's what the stars mean:

★ Recommended
★★ Highly Recommended
★★★ A must! Don't miss!

CONTENTS

LIST OF MAPS

ABOUT THE AUTHORS

Stephen Brewer has been savoring Italian pleasures ever since he sipped his first cappuccino while a student in Rome many, many years ago (togas had just gone out of fashion). He has written about Italy for many magazines and guidebooks and remains transported in equal measure by Bolognese cooking, Tuscan hillsides, the Bay of Naples, and the streets of Palermo.

Donald Strachan (Planning Chapter) is a travel journalist who has written about Italy for publications worldwide, including "National Geographic Traveler," "The Guardian," "Sunday Telegraph," CNN. com, and many others. He has also written several Italy guidebooks for Frommer's, including "Frommer's EasyGuide to Rome, Florence, and Venice." For more, see www.donaldstrachan.com.

1

INTRODUCTION

Sicily has been conquered, settled, and abandoned by dozens of civilizations, from the Phoenicians, Greeks, and Carthaginians in antiquity, to the Arabs, Berbers, Moors, and Normans in the Middle Ages, to the Spanish and Bourbons in the Renaissance, and finally, finally the (at least nominally) Italian modern era. It's an intricate and violent story that nonetheless left a fascinating legacy. Touring the relics of Sicily's tumultuous past can sometimes make you feel that you're visiting several different countries at once.

At 25,708 sq. km (9,926 sq. miles), Sicily is not only the largest island in the Mediterranean but also the largest region in Italy. This triangle-shaped land is home to the first known parliament in the western world (Palermo), the oldest continental tree (Sant'Alfio, near Catania), the highest and most active volcano in Europe (Mount Etna), and the most extensive archaeological park (Selinunte).

Though it's only separated from the mainland by the 4km-wide (2½ miles) Stretto di Messina, Sicily has a palpable, captivating sense of otherness. Some Sicilians will refer to a trip to the mainland as "going to Italy." The island offers the full package of Italian travel experiences: evocative towns, compelling art, impressive architecture, and ruins older than anything in Rome. Alongside the

PREVIOUS PAGE: **Agrigento at Sunset.**

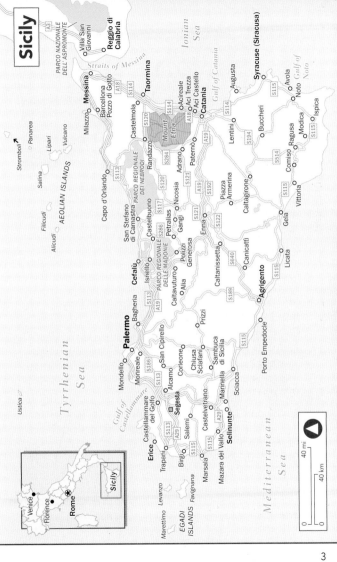

Sicily

Ancient ruins at Agrigento.

jewels of Sicily's glorious Classical past (Agrigento, Siracusa, Segesta, Tindari, Morgantina, Piazza Armerina) you'll see unique baroque cities rebuilt after devastating earthquakes (Catania, Noto, Scicli, Ragusa, and Modica)—and, sadly, also hideous postwar concrete monsters (Palermo, Catania, Messina, Agrigento).

The island's geographic palette goes from the sere, chalky southeast to the brooding slopes of Mount Etna to the brawny headlands of Palermo and the gentle, agricultural landscapes of the east—all surrounded by cobalt seas and beaches where you can swim from May to October. The colors and natural contrasts are shaped by the elements like nowhere else on Earth; African and Alpine fauna live spectacularly on the same island.

Then, of course, too, there are the Sicilians themselves: The descendants of Greek, Carthaginian, Roman Vandal, Arab, Norman, and Spanish conquerors. They can be welcoming yet suspicious, taciturn and at the same time garrulous, deeply tied to traditions yet always yearning to break away from distasteful precedents. True to stereotypes, Sicilians are a passionate people, and their warmth can make even everyday transactions memorable.

Thousands of years of domination may have created stark contradictions, but they have left an archaeological, cultural, and culinary legacy like no other in this world. In Goethe's words, "The key to it all is here."

Don't Leave Sicily Without . . .

TEMPTING FATE ON AN ACTIVE VOLCANO   Massive Mount Etna (p. 80) dominates Sicily's eastern coast and still rumbles and spews quite frequently, sometimes erupting in spectacular fashion. A trek to its 3,326m (10,910-ft. (3,326 m) summit—by cable car, off-road vehicle, or your own two feet—is a thrilling must-do. Off the northern coast of Sicily, the extremely active volcanic island of Stromboli (p. 68) never stops emitting a tall column of smoke, and nighttime excursions to see lava spurts at the crater (only offered when conditions are safe) are also an unforgettable experience.

DOING JUSTICE TO PALERMO   The sensory overload in Sicily's capital can be overwhelming. It's the ultimate city of contrasts—where Norman palaces stand

Palermo's grand cathedral.

The seaside town of Scopello.

The Teatro Massimo in Palermo.

triumphant around the corner from apartment buildings still heavily scarred by World War II bombing—and it reveals its delights slowly, like a morphine drip.

GOING GREEK   Sicily has the finest ancient Greek ruins outside of Greece, and they make a satisfying contrast to all the Roman ruins you'll be seeing in the rest of Italy. Agrigento's Valley of the Temples (p. 123), on the island's southern flank, is a world-class archaeological site, where the skeletons of seven Doric temples stand along an atmospheric ridge with almond trees. The Greco-Roman Theater in Taormina may have the most stunning natural setting of all ancient playhouses. Siracusa's lush archaeological park is a delight to explore, from the Greek theater to the "Ear of Dionysius" cave. Several other important 2,500-year-old sites, like the temples at Segesta and Selinunte, round out the mix.

GETTING OUT ON THE WATER   The seas that surround Sicily are today among the most unspoiled that Italy has to offer. From the sandy beaches at Cefalù and Fontane Bianche (Siracusa) or the dramatic coves near Taormina, don't miss a chance to go for a dip in these sparkling waters.

SPIKING YOUR BLOOD SUGAR Throw that diet out the window, because Sicily has some otherworldly dolci (sweets) that are near impossible to find done properly anywhere else. Number one on the list is the cannolo (you may know it better by the plural form, cannoli), whose name means "little tube." It's a fried pastry shell filled with sweet and creamy mascarpone, vanilla, and bits of chocolate and sometimes pistachio. Sicily's other sweet par excellence, cassata—sponge cake with ricotta filling and marzipan or chocolate frosting—goes back 1,000 years to when the Arabs ruled Sicily. Most Sicilian towns and provinces have their own specialties, so stop into the local *pasticceria* (pastry shop) to sample the local treats.

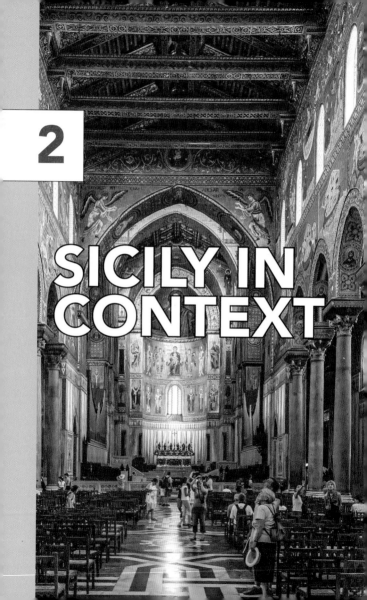

2

SICILY IN CONTEXT

As with any destination, a little background reading can help you to understand more. Many Italy stereotypes are accurate—children are fussed over wherever they go, food and soccer are like religion, the north–south divide is alive and well, bureaucracy is a frustrating feature of daily life. Some are wide of the mark—not every Italian you meet will be open and effusive. Occasionally they do taciturn pretty well, too.

The most important thing to remember is that, for a land so steeped in history—3 millennia and counting—Italy has only a short history *as a country*. In 2011 it celebrated its 150th birthday. Prior to 1861, the map of the peninsula was in constant flux. And you'll find Sicily to be very different than other parts of Italy.

A BRIEF HISTORY OF SICILY

Sicily's tenuous position—strung between North Africa and the European mainland, just 160km (100 miles) from Cap Bon in Tunisia on one side and 3km (2 miles) from Calabria in Italy on the other—has made it a natural stepping stone for settlers and invaders throughout its long history. The earliest-known

FACING PAGE: **Cathedral Santa Maria Nuova of Monreale.**

inhabitants were the Sicanians, who most likely came from somewhere in the eastern Mediterranean in the 3rd millennium B.C. A Latin people called the Sikels arrived around 1200 B.C., and the Elymians from Asia Minor came to the island around 1100 B.C. The merging of these three early peoples formed the basis for the uniquely Sicilian ethnicity; it was added to, of course, over the next 3,000 years.

Sicily's Hellenistic cities—**Siracusa**, **Catania**, and **Messina**—were founded in the 6th through 8th centuries B.C. by the Greeks, who later built vast temples all over the island, which still stand at Agrigento, Segesta, and Selinunte. Throughout the 4th and 5th centuries B.C., the Carthaginians of North Africa fought the Greeks—and later the Romans—for control and turned the island into a bloody battlefield. After the fall of Rome, Sicily underwent many occupations before returning to the Arabs, or Saracens, in the 9th century, when Islam became the official religion.

The Arab rulers tolerated Christianity and Judaism on Sicily.

When the Normans wrested control of the island from the Saracens in the 11th century, Sicily began its Golden Age, throughout which its ancient Greek, Arab, and Byzantine influences would blend together and eventually define so much of its character. Sicily fell to the French in the 13th

A windmill in Marsala.

century and was repeatedly sacked and oppressed for the next several hundred years. The Sicilians eventually reacted to this oppression by forming their own secret society, which they called Mafia, a term derived from the Arabic word for "refuge." In the 1700s, this secret society, by then also known as the Cosa Nostra ("our thing"), began distributing a picture of a black hand, which was as a formal request for protection money. Those who didn't pay faced misfortune—or worse. (The Cosa Nostra is still very much a force in Sicily today, though it's unlikely that you'll be aware of its presence. They do not target tourists.)

By the 19th century, Sicily and Naples formed a sovereign kingdom called the "Two Sicilies," which unified with Italy in 1861. After unification, Sicily became part of Italy's "poor south," and its problems were largely ignored by the Italian government.

Today Sicily exists primarily as an agricultural region, its economy heavily subsidized by tourism and profits manipulated by an ever-efficient Mafia. A growing premier wine industry is starting to get international attention. Five million people live on Sicily; 1,300,000 of them are in Palermo.

One delight in visiting Sicily is viewing its many pasts, one layer upon the other. Phoenician ruins on the western coast (now anchored by modern-day Palermo) sit below Norman-Arab castles. In Siracusa, a splendid baroque cathedral lies directly on top of a Greek temple. And in Corleone, the hill town and real-life Mafia stronghold that inspired the name of the famous "Godfather" character, the main bus terminus is on Piazza delle Vittime della Mafia (Mafia Victims' Square).

ITALY TODAY

The big Italian news for many travelers is the recent favorable movement in exchange rates. In 2014, the US dollar/euro exchange rate at $1.37. At time of writing, it's $1.06. Everything in Italy just became 22% cheaper for visitors from across the Atlantic. (The Canadian dollar has moved less dramatically, but still in the right direction—from $1.51 to $1.33.) So, congratulations: You picked a good time to visit.

Many Italians have not been so lucky. One reason for the euro's plunge is a stubbornly slow European recovery from the global financial crisis—known here as the *Crisi*. It had a disastrous effect on Italy's economy, causing the deepest recession since World War II. Public debt had grown to alarming levels—as high as 1,900 billion euros—and for more than a decade economic growth has been slow. As a result, 2011 and 2012 saw Italy pitched into the center of a European banking crisis, which almost brought about the collapse of the euro. By 2015, many Italians were beginning to see light at the end of their dark economic tunnel—a little, at least.

Populism has become a feature of national politics. A party led by comedian Beppe Grillo—the *MoVimento 5 Stelle* (Five

Piazza San Domenico in Palermo.

Star Movement)—polled around a quarter of the vote in 2013 elections. By early 2014, in the postelectoral shakedown, former Florence mayor Matteo Renzi became Italy's youngest prime minister—at 39 years of age—heading a coalition of the center-left led by his Democratic Party (PD). Among his first significant acts was to name a governing cabinet made up of equal numbers of men and women, a ratio unprecedented in Italy. Opinion polling through mid-2015 showed Italians still favoring Renzi's reformism over rivals' policies.

Italy's population is aging, and a youth vacuum is being filled by immigrants, especially those from Eastern Europe, notably Romania (whose language is similar to Italian) and Albania, as well as from North Africa. Italy doesn't have the colonial experience of Britain and France, or the "melting pot" history of the New World; tensions were inevitable, and discrimination is a daily fact of life for many minorities. Change is coming—in 2013, Cécile Kyenge became Italy's first black government minister, and black footballer Mario Balotelli is one of the country's biggest sports stars. But it is coming too slowly for some.

A "brain drain" continues to push young Italians to seek opportunities abroad. The problem is especially bad in rural communities and on the islands, where the old maxim, "it's not what you know, it's who you know," applies more strongly than ever in these straitened times. By 2015, however, indicators suggested the worst of Italy's economic turmoil might be behind it. From top to toe, highlands to islands, fingers are firmly crossed that the good times are coming round again.

WHEN TO GO

The best months for traveling in Sicily are from **April to June** and **mid-September to October**—temperatures are usually comfortable, rural colors are richer, and the crowds aren't too intense (except around Easter). From **July through early September** the country's holiday spots teem with visitors.

August is the worst month in most places: Not only does it get uncomfortably hot, muggy, and crowded, but seemingly the entire country goes on vacation, at least from August 15 onward—and many Italians take off the entire month. Many family-run hotels, restaurants, and shops are closed (except at the spas, beaches, and islands, where most Italians head). Paradoxically, you will have many urban places almost to yourself if you visit in August. Just be aware that many fashionable restaurants and nightspots are closed for the whole month.

From **late October to Easter,** many attractions operate on shorter (sometimes *much* shorter) winter hours, and some hotels are closed for renovation or redecoration, though that is less likely if you are visiting the cities. Many family-run restaurants take a week or two off sometime between **November and February;** spa and beach destinations become padlocked ghost towns.

Calamosche beach.

cuisine **IN SICILY**

Italians know how to cook—just ask one. But be sure to leave plenty of time: Once an Italian starts talking food, it's a while before they pause for breath. Italy doesn't really have a unified national cuisine; it's more a loose grouping of regional cuisines that share a few staples, notably pasta, bread, tomatoes, and pig meat cured in many ways.

Sicily has a distinctive cuisine, with strong flavors and aromatic sauces. One staple is *pasta con le sarde* (with pine nuts, wild fennel, spices, chopped sardines, and olive oil). In fact, fish is good and fresh pretty much everywhere (local swordfish is excellent). Desserts and homemade pastries include *cannoli*, cylindrical pastry cases stuffed with ricotta and candied fruit (or chocolate). Sicilian *gelato* is among the best in Italy.

Weather

It's warm all over Italy in summer; it can be very hot in Sicily.

The rainiest months are usually October and November.

Public Holidays

Offices, government buildings (though not usually tourist offices), and shops in Italy are generally closed on: January 1 (*Capodanno,* or New Year); January 6 (*La Befana,* or Epiphany); Easter Sunday (*Pasqua*); Easter Monday (*Pasquetta*); April 25 (Liberation Day); May 1 (*Festa del Lavoro,* or Labor Day); June 2 (*Festa della Repubblica,* or Republic Day); August 15 (*Ferragosto,* or the Assumption of the Virgin); November 1 (All Saints' Day); December 8 (*L'Immacolata,* or the

Immaculate Conception); December 25 (*Natale*, Christmas Day); December 26 (*Santo Stefano*, or St. Stephen's Day). You'll also often find businesses closed for the annual daylong celebration dedicated to the local saint (for example, on January 31 in San Gimignano, Tuscany).

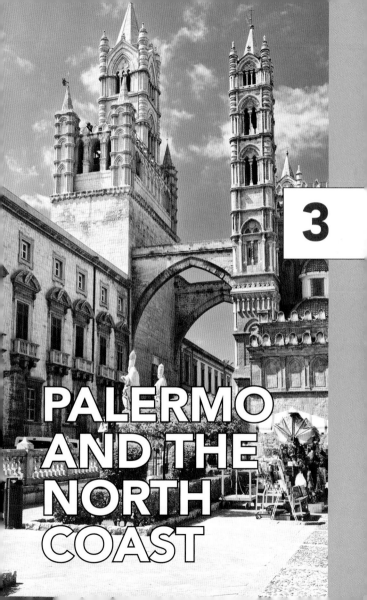

3

PALERMO
AND THE
NORTH
COAST

Boisterous, clamorous Palermo is one of Italy's most fascinating and treasure-laden cities. The island's capital is also within easy reach of other intriguing places that include Monreale, with shimmering mosaics in its medieval cathedral, the Greek ruins at Segesta, and Cefalù, a fishing village turned resort.

PALERMO ★★★

233km (145 miles) W of Messina, 721km (447 miles) S of Naples, 934km (579 miles) S of Rome

In Palermo, street markets evoke Middle Eastern souks, and famous monuments bear the exotic artistic signature of the Arab-Norman 12th century, when Palermo was one of Europe's greatest cultural and intellectual centers. The city is Sicily's largest port, its capital, and a jumble of contradiction. Parts of some neighborhoods remain bombed out and not yet rebuilt from World War II; unemployment, poverty, traffic, crime, and crowding are rampant. Yet Palermo boasts some of the greatest sights and museums in Italy, and looming over it all is crown-shaped Monte Pellegrino, what Goethe called "the most beautiful headland on earth."

Essentials

By Air   Flights arrive at Palermo's dramatically situated **Falcone-Borsellino airport** (aka Punta Raisi;

PREVIOUS PAGE: **The Cathedral of Palermo erected in 1185.**

www.gesap.it; ✆ **091-7020273**), on the sea among tall headlands 25km (16 miles) northwest of the city center (the airport is named for the two anti-Mafia magistrates who were assassinated in the early 1990s). Palermo is well served by flights from all over Italy and many European cities. In summer, a few weekly non-stop flights operated by Meridiana (www.meridiana.it; ✆ **0789 52682** in Italy, **718-751-4499** in U.S.) also arrive from New York. All the major rental car companies have operations here, although if you drive into Palermo with a rental car, get clear directions and parking information from your hotel. An easier way to reach the center from the airport is with the shuttle bus run by **Prestia e Comandè** (✆ **091-580457**). The buses depart every half-hour from 5am to 11pm; the trip takes 45 minutes and costs 7€ one-way. In central Palermo, the bus stops at the main train station, at Via Emerico Amari (port), and at Teatro Politeama. There's also a direct train called the **Trinacria Express** (www.trenitalia.com; ✆ **091-7044007;** 1 hr.; 6€) from Palermo airport to Palermo central station. Taxis are plentiful but expensive; expect to pay about 50€ from the airport to town.

By Bus　　Palermo is the terminus for bus routes to all parts of Sicily. Bus travel in Sicily is excellent, with good connections between most cities. Buses are clean and modern, with comfortable upholstered seats, air-conditioning, and smooth suspensions. The main bus companies in Sicily are **Interbus** (www.interbus.it; ✆ **091-6167919;** also goes by the names **Etna Trasporti, Segesta,** and **Sicilbus,** depending on which part of Sicily you're in), and **Cuffaro** (www.

cuffaro.info; ✆ **091-6161510**), which operates buses between Palermo and Agrigento. Buses arrive at a depot adjacent to the train station.

By Car If you're planning to drive down from Naples or Rome, prepare yourself for a long ride: 721km (448 miles) south from Naples or 934km (580 miles) south from Rome. You'll cross the 5km-wide (3-miles) Stretto di Messina (Strait of Messina) on one of the many ferries that operate between the Calabrian port of **Villa San Giovanni** (just north of Reggio Calabria, essentially the "toe" of the Italian peninsula's boot shape) and the Sicilian city of **Messina**. From Messina, it's a straight shot west to Palermo (233km/145 miles; about 2 hr.) on the A20 autostrada. Sicilian

A bird's eye view of Palermo.

roads, as in the rest of Italy, are generally signposted well. Before taking the wheel acquire a good road map (*carta stradale*), such as that published by Touring Editore, available at newsstands and bookshops.

By Train   Trains to Palermo are operated by Italy's national rail company, **Ferrovie dello Stato** (www.trenitalia.com). The trains from mainland Italy come down from Rome, Naples, and other Italian cities through Calabria and across the Strait of Messina to Sicily on ferries equipped with railroad tracks on the cargo deck. It's a novel way to arrive in Sicily. Travel time between Naples and Palermo is 9–10 hrs. All trains come into Palermo Stazione Centrale, just south of the historic center. Note that passenger rail service on the island is generally spotty and slow, with limited routes and antiquated, dirty coaches. The bus is almost always a better option everywhere except along the north coast between Palermo and Messina.

By Sea   Palermo's large port is served by passenger ferries from the Italian mainland cities of Naples, Civitavecchia (near Rome), Livorno, Genova, and from the Sardinian city of Cagliari. Nearly all of these are nighttime crossings, departing between 7pm and 9pm and arriving the next morning between 6am and 8am. Some of these ferries are tricked out like miniature cruise ships, with swimming pools, beauty salons, discos, gyms, and presidential suites. Ferries from Naples are the most numerous, operating daily year-round. The Naples-Palermo route is run by **SNAV** (www.snav.it; ✆ **081-4285555**) and **Tirrenia Lines** (www.tirrenia.it; ✆ **892123** or 02-26302803). With either company, the ferry trip takes 11 hours, although there is also a faster, more expensive daytime hydrofoil service that takes 6 hours (summer only). From Civitavecchia, which is the port that cruise ships use when visiting Rome, **Grandi Navi Veloci** (www.gnv.it; © **010/2094591**) has ferries to Palermo that depart at 8pm, arriving in Palermo the next morning at 8am. Schedules vary depending on weather conditions, so always call on the day of departure even if you've already confirmed your reservation the day before.

VISITOR INFORMATION   Official **tourist information offices** are located at Falcone-Borsellino (Punta Raisi) airport (© **091-591698;** Mon–Sat 8:30am–7:30pm), and in the city center at Piazza Castelnuovo 35 (© **091-6058351;** Mon–Fri 8:30am–2pm and 2:30–6:30pm). The website of Palermo's tourism board is www.palermotourism.com.

SAFETY   Palermo is home to some of the most skilled pickpockets on the continent. Don't flaunt expensive jewelry, cameras, or wads of bills. Women who carry handbags are especially vulnerable to purse snatchers on Vespas. Police squads operate mobile centers throughout the town to help combat street crime.

Neighborhoods in Brief

Palermo is divided into four historical districts, or *mandamenti,* that spread out from **Quattro Canti,** or Four Corners. The actual name of the square is Piazza Vigliena, after the viceroy who commissioned it, and it marks the intersection of **Via Maqueda** (which runs north–south) and **Corso Vittorio Emanuele** (which runs east–west, east toward the seafront from here). The square is also known as Theater of the Sun,

Palermo

To the Giardino Inglese

Via Dante
Via della Libertà
Via Houel
Piazza Castelnuovo
Teatro Politeama
Piazza Sturzo
Via Emerico Amari
Via Principe di Belmonte
Pza. Florio
Via Mariano Stabile
Via Ruggero Settimo
Via Francesco Crispi
Via del Mare
Via Sammuzzo

Piazza Sant'Oliva
Via P. Aragona
NEW CITY ❶

Via Goethe
Via Polara
Piazza di Giustizia
Via Volturno
Teatro Massimo
Piazza Verdi ❷
Via Cavour
Via Squarcialupo ❸
Via Flippo Patti

Via Sant' Amedeo
Via Sant' Agostino
Capo Market
Via Bandiera
Chiesa di S. Domenico ❹
Piazza S. Domenico
Vucciria Market
La Cala

Corso Alberto
Via del Celso
Maqueda
Emanuele ❺
Piazza Marina
Giardino Garibaldi

Duomo ❶❼
OLD CENTER
Via Vittorio
Quattro Canti ❶❻ ❻
Piazza Pretoria ❶❺
❾ **San Francesco d'Assisi** ❽ ❼
Piazza Magione
Piazza Marina

Pal. dei Normanni ←❶❽
Villa Bonanno
Piazza della Vittoria
Via Porta di Castro
Cappella Palatina ❶❾
Via Roma
Piazza Rivoluzione ❿ ⓫ ⓬

❷⓪
Via dei Benedettini
Via Antonino Mongitore
Via Albergheria
Ballarò Market
V. del Bosco
Via Divisi
Via Alloro ⓭
Santa Teresa

Corso Tukory
Via Garibaldi
Piazza Rivoluzione
LA KALSA
Via Lincoln ⓮

0 — 1/4 mi
0 — 250 m

Piazza G. Cesare
Stazione Centrale

because at any given time of day, the sun will shine on one of the four corners.

ALBERGHERIA   Located southwest of the Quattro Canti, this is the oldest of the four *mandamenti;* it is also known as the mandamento Palazzo Reale because the Phoenicians first laid the foundations of what would become the royal place on the highest part of the city. These were the streets roamed by the 18th-century soothsayer and charlatan Giuseppe Balsamo (aka Count Cagliostro), an adventurer, traveler, swindler, forger, and thief who spent time in the Bastille after allegedly stealing a diamond necklace from Marie Antoinette; he was finally tried by the Inquisition and died in a Roman prison. The Albergheria is filled with tiny, dimly lit alleyways barely wide enough for a person to walk along, and decaying buildings in dire need of repair; it is unsavory in some patches, despite the ever-growing presence of cafes and eateries. Still, there are some very exquisite corners—especially the splendid Piazza Bologni, with is noble palaces and a statue of Charles V, and the historic market **Il Ballarò** extending from Piazza Bologni to Corso Tukory.

IL CAPO   The northwestern neighborhood, enclosed within Via Maqueda, Corso Vittorio Emanuele, Via Papireto and Via Volturno, has a warren of tiny, winding streets and alleyways spread out behind the Teatro Massimo. At its heart is the largest and the most bazaarlike of Palermo's markets, also called **Il Capo.** The Capo was once the headquarters of the secret society of the Beati Paoli, the legendary sect that robbed from the rich and gave to the poor; pickpockets still adhere to this age-old principle, so watch your wallet.

Do Some Market Research

You can't do justice to Palermo without swinging through one of its street markets. Nowhere is Palermo's multicultural pedigree more evident than at the stalls of the sadly declining **La Vucciria** (on Via Argenteria, north of Via Vittorio Emanuele and east of Via Roma), **Ballarò** (in Piazza Ballarò), and **Capo** (from Via Porta Carini south toward the cathedral). These open-air markets go on for blocks and blocks, hawking everything from spices to seafood to sides of beef to toilet paper to handicrafts to electronics. Ballarò and Capo, west and north of the train station, are where more real Palermitans shop. Delve even deeper into Palermo's market culture at the neighborhood **Borgo Vecchio** market (along Via Ettore Ximenes to Via Principe di Scordia) in the newer part of the city, northwest of Piazza Politeama. Antiques vendors with many unusual buys lie along the Piazza Peranni, off Corso Vittorio Emanuele.

CASTELLAMMARE Owing its name to the castle that once overlooked the sea, this northeastern quadrant is bordered by Corso Vittorio Emanuele, Via Cavour, Via Roma, and Via Crispi. Though heavily bombed by the Allies during 1943, the neighborhood houses some spectacular palazzi and churches, such as the **Oratorio del Rosario di Santa Cita** and the **Oratorio di San Lorenzo** (p. 32). The centuries-old market **La Vucciria,** once the beating heart of Palermo, is located here (see p. 27). Though only a smattering of its vibrancy remains, you'll still see butcher shops called *carnizzerie,* fishmongers scaring shoppers with large heads of swordfish, precarious houses that look as though they might crumble any time (some have in recent years), and tiny, hole-in-the-wall eateries that may seem shady and improvised, but are often excellent.

LA KALSA   A thousand years ago, Arabs settled the southeast quadrant, La Kalsa, which is bounded by Via Lincoln, Via Roma, Corso Vittorio Emanuele, and the Foro Italico. The neighborhood still has an exotic feel to it. Time was, even 10 years ago, when the quarter was so insalubrious that walking down the narrow lanes was risky business. It's still wise to avoid some emptier areas after dark, though these are rather rare these days, as restaurants and bars have opened in old *palazzi*.

NEW CITY   As you head north along Via Maqueda, the streets grow broader but also more nondescript. The monumental **Teatro Massimo**, at Piazza Verdi, roughly marks the division between the Old City and the New City. Via Maqueda becomes Via Ruggero Séttimo as it heads north through the modern town, emptying into the massive double squares at Piazza Politeama, site of the **Teatro Politeama Garibaldi.** North of the square is Palermo's swankiest street, **Viale della Libertà,** running up toward Giardino Inglese (the English Gardens). This is the area where the Art Nouveau movement triumphed in the city, as is still visible in the kiosks at Piazza Castelnuovo and in Piazza Verdi, but many of these priceless edifices were torn down by unscrupulous builders to make way for ugly cement behemoths that mar the elegance of the neighborhood.

Exploring Palermo

Most of everything you want to see is within walking distance of the Quattro Canti, where Via Maqueda meets Via Vittorio Emanuele.

Catacombs of the Capuchins (Catacombe dei Cappuccini) ★ CEMETERY

In 1599, the occupants of the adjoining Capuchin monastery discovered that the bodies of the brothers they placed in their catacombs soon became naturally mummified, and Sicilians began demanding to be buried along with them. In these chambers, the corpses of some 8,000 people in various stages of preservation now hang from walls and recline in open caskets. It would be easy to write the spectacle off as eerie (which it certainly is) or even a bit vampy, but for the deceased and the loved ones they left behind, a spot here provided a bit of comforting immortality. Wearing their Sunday best, the dead are grouped according to sex and rank—men, women, virgins, priests, nobles, professors (possibly including the painter Velasquez, though his presence here is questionable), and children. This last grouping includes the most recent resident, 2-year-old Rosalia Lombardo, who died in 1920 and whom locals have dubbed "Sleeping Beauty." Giuseppe Tommasi, prince of Lampedusa and author of one of the best-known works of Sicilian literature, *The Leopard*, was buried in the cemetery next to the catacombs in 1957. His great-grandmother, the model for the princess in the novel, is in the catacombs.

Capuchins Monastery, Piazza Cappuccini 1. ✆ **091-212117.** Admission 3€. Daily 9am–noon and 3–5pm (until 7pm in summer). Closed holidays. Bus: 327.

Chiesa della Martorana/San Cataldo ★★ CHURCH

These two Norman churches stand side by side, separated by a little tropical garden. George of Antioch, Roger II's Greek admiral, founded Santa Maria dell'Ammiraglio in 1141; the church was later renamed **Chiesa della Martorana** for Eloisa Martorana, who

Shopping at a local market in Palermo.

founded a nearby Benedictine convent. The nuns gained the everlasting appreciation of Palermitans when they invented marzipan, and *frutta di Martorana*—sweets in which marzipan is fashioned into the shape of little fruits—has outlived the order. George of Antioch, for his part, had a love of Byzantine mosaics and hired the North African craftsmen who had just completed their work on the **Cappella Palatina** (see p. 620) to also cover this church's walls, pillars, and floors with stunning mosaics in deep hues of ivory, green, azure, red, and gold. Christ crowns Roger II, George appears in a Byzantine robe, and Christ appears again in the dome, surrounded by angels. The Arab geographer/traveler Ibn Jubayr visited Palermo in

1166 and called the church "the most beautiful monument in the world." In 1266 Sicilian nobles met here and agreed to offer the crown to Peter of Aragon, ending a bloody uprising against French rule known as the Sicilian Vespers. A baroque redo has rendered the interior a little less transporting than it was then, but it's still beautiful.

Maio of Bari, chancellor to William I, began the tiny **Chiesa di San Cataldo** next door in 1154, but he died before it was completed in 1160, so the church was left unfinished. The red domes and the lacy crenellation around the tops of the walls are decidedly Moorish, while the stone interior, with three little cupolas over the nave, evoke the Middle Ages—all the more so since traces were removed of the church's use over the years as a hospital and post office.

Adjoining Piazza Pretoria is graced with the 16th-century Fontana Pretoria, where nymphs, god, and goddesses romp in a huge basin. Their nakedness inspired Palermians to call the exuberant assemblage the "Fountain of Shame," as it's been known ever since.

Piazza Bellini 2, adjacent to Piazza Pretoria. © **091-6161692.** La Martorana: Free admission. Mon–Sat 9:30am–1pm and 3:30–6:30pm; Sun 8:30am–1pm. San Cataldo: 2€. Tues–Fri 9am–5pm; Sat–Sun 9am–1pm. Bus: 101 or 102.

Duomo ★ CATHEDRAL   All those who came, saw, and conquered in Palermo left their mark on this cathedral, an architectural pastiche that lies somewhere between exquisite and eyesore. It is, however, noble enough as befits the final resting place of Roger II, the first king of Sicily, who died in 1154, and other Norman–Swabian royalty. Neapolitan architect Ferdinando

THE oratories OF GIACOMO SERPOTTA

Some of Palermo's most delightful places of worship are oratories, private chapels funded by private societies and guilds and usually connected to a larger church. Giacomo Serpotta, a native master of sculpting in stucco, decorated several oratorios in the early 18th century. Most are open Monday through Friday 10am to 1pm and 3 to 6pm, Saturday 10am to 1pm, though hours vary. You'll be charged 2€ admission, but your ticket is good at at least one other oratory.

Serpotta was a member of the Society of the Holy Rosary, and he decorated the society's **Oratorio del Rosario di San Domenico** (Via dei Bambinai; ✆ **091-332779**) with his delightfully expressive *putti* (cherubs), who are locked forever in a playground of happy antics. His 3-D reliefs depict everything from the Allegories of the Virtues to the Apocalypse of St. John to a writhing "Devil Falling from Heaven." Anthony van Dyck, the Dutch master who spent time in Palermo in the 1620s, did the "Madonna of the Rosary" over the high altar.

Serpotta also worked on the **Oratorio di San Lorenzo**

Fuga began a restoration in 1771 that gave the exterior and the interior an all-encompassing neoclassical style, adding a cupola that sticks out like a sore thumb on the original Norman design. With a little attention you can pick out some of the original elements: four impressive campaniles (bell towers) from the 14th century; the middle portal from the 15th century; and the south and north porticos from the 15th and 16th centuries. Take note of the column on the left of the south portico: It

(Via dell'Immacolatella; ☏ **091-332779**) between 1698 and 1710, creating panels relating the details of the lives of St. Francis and St. Lawrence to create what critics have admiringly called "a cave of white coral." Some of the most expressive of the stuccoes depict the martyrdom of Lawrence, who was roasted to death and nonchalantly informed his tormentors, "I'm well done. Turn me over." Among the reliefs are serene-looking statues of the Virtues, amid them naked *putti* romping gaily. Caravaggio's last large painting, a "Nativity," once hung over the altar, but it was stolen in 1969 and never recovered.

The all-white **Oratorio del Rosario di Santa Cita** (Via Valverde 3; ☏ **091-332779**) houses Serpotta's crowning achievement, a detailed relief of the Battle of Lepanto, in which a coalition of European states defeated the Turks, more or less preventing the expansion of the Ottoman Empire into Western Europe. Serpotta's cherubs, oblivious to international affairs, romp up and down the walls and climb onto window frames.

was recycled from a mosque and is inscribed with a verse from the Koran.

Piazza Cattedrale. ☏ **091-334373.** Duomo: free admission; crypt and treasury: 1€ each. Mon–Sat 9:30am–1:30pm and 2:30–5:30pm. Bus: 101, 104, 105, 107, or 139.

Galleria Regionale della Sicilia (Regional Gallery)/Palazzo Abatellis ★★★ MUSEUM Center stage at this fine collection is the late–15th century *palazzo* that houses it, built around two courtyards and

Ancient mosaics are a highlight of the Regional Archeological Museum.

beautifully restored in the 1950s. On display is an array of the arts in Sicily from the 13th to the 18th centuries, though it's hard to get beyond the gallery's most celebrated work, the **"Trionfo della Morte" ("Triumph of Death").** Dating from 1449 and of uncertain attribution, this huge study in black and gray is prominently displayed in a two-story ground-floor gallery (once you've looked at it up close, climb the stairs to the balcony for an overview). Death has never looked worse—a fearsome skeletal demon astride an undernourished steed, brandishing a scythe as he leaps over his victims (allegedly members of Palermo aristocracy, who were none too pleased with the portrayal). The painter is believed to have depicted himself in the fresco, seen with an apprentice praying in vain for release from the horrors of Death; the poor and hungry, looking on from the side, have escaped such a gruesome fate for the time being. The precision of this astonishing work, including details of the horse's nostrils and the men and women in the full flush of their youth, juxtaposed against such darkness, suggests the Surrealism movement that came to the fore 400 years later.

The second masterpiece of the gallery, in room 4, is a refreshing antidote, and also quite modern-looking: the white-marble, slanted-eyed bust of **"Eleonora di Aragona,"** by Francesco Laurana. The Dalmatian-born sculptor was in Sicily from 1466 to 1471, and he captured this likeness of Eleanor, daughter of King Ferdinand I of Naples, shortly before she married Ercole d'Este and became the duchess of Ferrara. Of the Sicilian artists on display, Antonello da Messina stands out, with an "Annunciation" in room 11. (It is one of the two Annunciations he painted; the other is at the Bellomo museum in Siracusa, see p. 603). This one is probably the artist's most famous work, completed in 1476 in Venice. He depicts the Virgin as an adolescent girl, sitting at a desk with a devotional book in front of her, clasping her cloak modestly to her chest. She raises her hand, seemingly to us viewers but probably to Gabriel, who has just delivered the news that she is to be the mother of the son of God. Considering that news, her expression is remarkably serene. This is one of the most lovely and calming works anywhere.

Via Alloro 4, Palazzo Abatellis. ℂ **091-6230011.** Admission 8€ adults, 4€ children. Tues–Sun 9am–1:30pm and 2:30–6:30pm. Bus: 103, 105, or 139.

Museo Archeologico Regionale "Antonino Salinas" (Regional Archaeological Museum) ★★★

The first thing to know about this stunning collection of antiquities is that you may not see it, as the museum was closed indefinitely in 2011 for a much-needed renovation. In the interim, a few pieces are shown in ground-floor galleries and the courtyard. When it's operating at full swing, the former convent of the Filippini, built around a lovely cloister, displays a head-spinning repository of artifacts from the island's many inhabitants and invaders: Phoenicians, Greeks, Saracens, and Romans. The museum's most important treasures are metopes (temple friezes) from once-great Selinunte on the southern coast. Sumptuous, detailed marbles depict Perseus slaying Medusa, the Rape of Europa by Zeus, Actaeon being transformed into a stag, and other scenes that bring these myths vividly to life. Among the other artifacts—anchors from Punic warships, mirrors used by the Etruscans, and a joyful Roman statue of "Satyr Filling a Drinking Cup"—is a rare Egyptian find: The **Pietra di Palermo** (Palermo Stone), a black stone slab dating from 2700 B.C. that is known as the Rosetta stone of Sicily. Discovered in Egypt in the 19th century, it was in transit for the British Museum in London when it was shuffled off to the corners of a Palermo dock. The hieroglyphics reveal the inscriber's attention to detail: a list of pharaohs, details of the delivery of 40 shiploads of cedarwood to Snefru, and flood levels of the Nile.

Piazza Olivella 24. ⓒ **091-6116805.** Closed temporarily. Admission 4€ adults, 2€ children 18 and under. Tues–Fri 8:30am–1:30pm and 2:30–6:30pm; Sat–Sun and holidays 8:30am–1:30pm. Bus: 101, 102, 103, 104, 107, or Linea Rossa.

Palazzo dei Normanni ★★ and Cappella Palatina ★★★ PALACE The cultural influences of Sicily collide in this palace, which dates back to the 8th century B.C., when Punic administrators set up an outpost in the highest part of the city. In the 9th century A.D. the Arabs built a palace on the spot for their emirs and their harems, and in the 12th century the Normans turned what was essentially a fortress into a sumptuous royal residence. Here Frederick II presided over the early 13th-century court of minstrels and literati that founded the Schola Poetica Siciliana, which marked the birth of Italian literature. Spanish viceroys took up residence in the palace in 1555, and today most of the vast maze of rooms and grand halls houses the seat of Sicily's semiautonomous regional government.

Arab–Norman cultural influences intersect most spectacularly in the **Cappella Palatina**, a chapel covered in glittering Byzantine mosaics from 1130 to 1140. It was finished in time for the coronation of Roger II, who proved to be not only the most powerful of European kings but also the most enlightened. High in the cupola at the end of the apse is Christ Pantocrator (as usual in this iconic image, he holds the New Testament in his left hand and makes the gesture of blessing with his right hand). He is surrounded by saints and biblical characters, some interpreted a little less piously than usual—Adam and Eve happily

Mosaics in the Cappella Palatina.

munch on the forbidden fruit, and rather than showing any remorse for their act of defiance, they greedily reach for a second piece. Shame prevails in the next scene, when God steps in reproachfully and the naked couple covers themselves with leaves. The mosaics are vibrant in the soft light, and the effect is especially powerful in scenes depicting waters, as in the flood and the Baptism of Christ—in these, water appears actually to be shimmering.

More scenes appear on the wooden ceiling, done in a three-dimensional technique using small sections of carved wood, known in Arabic as *muqarnas*. A team of carpenters and painters was brought in from Egypt to create the playfully secular scenarios of dancers, musicians, hunters on horseback, drinkers, even banqueters in a harem. You'll see them best with binoculars or a telephoto lens.

Visits to the **Royal Apartments** are escorted, as this is a seat of government. Tours are almost always conducted in Italian; ask if there is an usher on duty who can speak English. The apartments are not open to the public when the Sicilian parliament is in session—meeting in the **Salone d'Ercole**, named for the mammoth 19th-century frescoes depicting the "Twelve Labours of Hercules" (pundits like to say this is apt decoration for legislators wading through government bureaucracy). The fairly pompous staterooms from the years of Spanish rule give way to earlier remnants, among them the **Sala dei Presidenti**; this stark chamber was hidden in the bowels of the palace for several centuries, completely unknown until 2002, when an earthquake knocked down one of the walls and unveiled an untouched, medieval relic. The **Torre Gioaria** (tower of the wind) is a harbinger of modern air-conditioning systems: A fountain in the middle of the tower (since removed) spouted water that cooled the breezes coming from the four hallways. In the Torre Gioaria is the Sala di Ruggero II, decorated with mosaics of nature and hunting scenes. Much less hospitable are the **Segrete**, or dungeons, where the cold stone walls are etched with primitive scenes of Norman warships. The otherwise enlightened Frederick II is said to have taken his interest in science to perverse lengths in these chambers, where he shut prisoners in casks to see whether or not their souls could be observed escaping through a small hole at the moment of death. He also imprisoned children, forbidding any interaction beyond sucking and bathing, to see if they would develop a natural language that would provide clues to the speech God gave Adam and Eve.

Frederick was fascinated by the stars and brought many astronomers and astrologers to his court. His Bourbon successors shared the interest and in 1790 added an astronomical observatory, still functioning, at the top of the **Torre Pisana**. From these heights in 1801 the priest Fra Giuseppe Piazza discovered Ceres, the first asteroid known to mankind.

Piazza del Parlamento. www.ars.sicilia.it. (℅) **091-626833.** Admission 8.50€, free for children 17 and under. Admission 7€ Tues–Thurs, when the Royal Apartments are closed due to Parliamentary meetings. Mon–Sat 8:15am–5pm; Sun 8:15am–12:15pm. Bus: 104, 105, 108, 109, 110, 118, 304, or 309.

San Giovanni degli Eremiti ★ CHURCH

Palermo's most romantic landmark is a simple affair, part Arab, part Norman, with five red domes atop a portico, a single nave, two small apses, and a squat tower. As befits the humble Spanish recluse it honors, St. John of the Hermits, the church is almost devoid of decoration, though the surrounding citrus blossoms and flowers imbue the modest structure with an otherworldy aura. Adding to the charms of the spot is a Norman cloister, with a Moorish cistern in the center, part of a Benedictine monastery that once stood here.

Via dei Benedettini 3. ⓒ **091-6515019.** Admission 6€ adults; 3€ students, seniors, and children. Tues–Sat 9am–1pm and 3–7pm; Sun 9am–6:30pm. Bus: 109 or 318.

Where to Stay

Palermo has some excellent hotels, with rates much lower than they are in Rome or Florence. For convenience and atmosphere, don't stay too far beyond the neighborhoods in the old center (see p. 24).

Ariston Hotel ★★   The sixth floor of an apartment building near Teatro Massimo is a welcoming retreat, with bright, airy rooms spread along a corridor off a comfortable lounge. Luxuries don't extend much beyond free coffee and tea, but the premises are spotless, owner/manager Giuseppe is a welcoming host, and the plain but pleasing furnishings and a smattering of modern art hit just the right tasteful notes—all making this place an excellent value.

Via Mariano Stabile 139. www.aristonpalermo.it.   ⓒ **091-3322434.** 8 units. 59€–75€ double. **Amenities:** Wi-Fi (free). Bus: 101.

The Ariston Hotel has a bustling cafe outside.

Butera 28 ★★★   The 17th-century Lanza Tomasi Palace, facing the seafront, is the home of Duke Gioacchino Lanza Tomasi, the adoptive son of Prince Giuseppe Tomasi di Lampedusa, author of one of the greatest works of modern Italian literature, *The Leopard*. The gracious duke and his charming wife, Nicoletta, have converted 12 apartments of their *palazzo* to short-stay apartments, filling them with family pieces and all the modern conveniences, including full kitchens and, every traveler's dream come true, washing machines. Apartments have one or two bedrooms; some have sea views and terraces, some are multilevel, and all have beautiful hardwood or tile floors and other detailing. The duchess also offers cooking classes, and she and the duke are on hand to provide a wealth of advice to help you get the most out of their beloved Palermo.

Via Butera 28. www.butera28.it. ℂ **333-316-5432.** 12 units. From 70€ double. **Amenities:** Kitchens, Wi-Fi (free). Bus: 103, 104, 105, 118, or 225.

Centrale Palace ★★   A wonderful location just steps off the Quattro Canti puts this much-redone yet still grand *palazzo* within easy reach of most sights. Public rooms, including a vast frescoed salon where breakfast is served, evoke the 1890s Belle Epoque age when the 17th-century *palazzo* was first converted to a hotel. The good-sized guest rooms above are comfortably functional, with some luxe touches like rich fabrics and mosaic-tiled bathrooms; double-pane windows in the front rooms keep the street noise at bay. A rooftop sun terrace offers a retreat from the city below, with views that extend across the rooftops to Monte Pellegrino. There's an airy dining

MEN OF dishonor

Members of the Sicilian Mafia (or "Men of Honor," as they like to be called) traditionally operated as a network of regional bosses who controlled individual towns by setting up puppet regimes of thoroughly corrupt officials. It was a sort of devil's bargain with the national Christian Democrat Party, which controlled Italy's government from World War II until 1993 and, despite its law-and-order rhetoric, tacitly left Cosa Nostra alone as long as the bosses got out the party vote.

The Cosa Nostra trafficked in illegal goods, of course, but until the 1960s and 1970s, its income was derived mainly from low-level protection rackets, funneling state money into its own pockets, and ensuring that public contracts were granted to fellow mafiosi (all reasons why Sicily has experienced unchecked industrialization and modern growth at the expense of its heritage and the welfare of its communities). But in the 1970s the younger generation of Mafia underbosses got into the highly lucrative heroin and cocaine trades, transforming the Sicilian Mafia into a world player on the international drug-trafficking circuit—and raking in the dough. This ignited a clandestine Mafia war that, throughout the late 1970s and 1980s, generated headlines of bloody Mafia hits. The new generation was

room up here, and you may want to linger well into a warm summer night.

Via Vittorio Emanuele 327 (at Via Maqueda). www.centrale palacehotel.it. ✆ **091-336666.** 104 units. 140€–271€ double. Some rates include buffet breakfast. Parking 18€. **Amenities:** 2 restaurants; bar; exercise room; sauna; room service; babysitting; Wi-Fi (free). Bus: 103, 104, or 105.

wiping out the old and turning the balance of power in their favor.

This situation gave rise to the first Mafia turncoats, disgruntled ex-bosses and rank-and-file stoolies who told their stories, first to police prefect Gen. Carlo Alberto Dalla Chiesa (assassinated 1982) and later to crusading magistrates Giovanni Falcone (killed May 23, 1992) and Paolo Borsellino (murdered July 19, 1992), who staged the "max-itrials" of mafiosi that sent hundreds to jail. The magistrates' 1992 murders, especially, drew public attention to the dishonorable methods of the new Mafia and, perhaps for the first time, began to stir true shame.

On a broad and culturally important scale, it is these young mafiosi, without a moral center or check on their powers, who have driven many Sicilians to at least secretly break the unwritten code of omertà, which translates as "homage" but means "silence," when faced with harboring or even tolerating a man of honor. The Mafia still exists in Palermo, the small towns south of it, and the provincial capitals of Catania, Trapani, and Agrigento. Throughout the rest of Sicily, its power has been slipping. The heroin trade is a far cry from construction schemes and protection money, and the Mafia is swiftly outliving its usefulness and its welcome.

Grand Hotel Piazza Borsa ★★ A conglomeration of three historic buildings seems to take in a bit of every part of Palermo's past—the banking floor and grand offices of the old stock exchange, a monastery, and a centuries-old *palazzo*. These elements come together atmospherically in surroundings that include a cloister, open-roofed atrium, paneled dining rooms, and frescoed salons. Guest rooms are a bit more businesslike, though large and plushly comfortable, with hardwood floors and furnishings that cross traditional with some contemporary flair; the best have balconies overlooking the surrounding churches and palaces. A spa and exercise area includes a sauna and steam room.

Via dei Cartari 18. www.piazzaborsa.com. ℂ **091-320075**. 103 units. 120€–200€ double. Rates include buffet breakfast. **Amenities:** Restaurant; bar; babysitting; concierge; Wi-Fi (free). Bus: 103, 104, 105, 118, or 225.

Hotel Porta Felice ★　It's a sign that the old Kalsa district is on the upswing that this elegant and subdued retreat has risen amid a once derelict block of buildings just off the seafront. Marble-floored public areas are coolly soothing, while guest rooms are sleekly contemporary, with just enough antique pieces and expanses of hardwood to suggest traditional comforts. A rooftop bar and terrace is a welcome refuge, while the downstairs health spa is geared to ultimate relaxation.

Via Butera 35. www.hotelportafelice.it. ℂ **091-617-5678.** 33 units. 130€–240€ double. Rates include buffet breakfast. **Amenities:** Bar; spa; Wi-Fi (free). Bus: 103, 104, 105, 118, or 225.

Where to Eat

Palermitans dine well on the fresh seafood and other bounty of the city markets, and they have a laudable appreciation for sweets. Legendary pastry shops like **Mazzara** (Via Generale Magliocco 19; ℂ **091-321443**) will fill you up with cassata, cannoli, *frutta martorana* (marzipan sweets), and gelato, while the opulent **Antico Caffè Spinnato** (Via Principe di Belmonte 115; www.spinnato.it; ℂ **091-583231**), established in 1860, is the place to linger over a pastry and coffee. While exploring the Kalsa quarter, you can satisfy a sweet tooth at **Ciccolateria Lorenzo,** near the

Palazzo Abatellis at Via Quattro Aprile 7 (© **091-840846;** closed Mon.), with a wonderful selection of cakes and the best hot chocolate in Palermo, and at **Antica Gelateria Patricola,** on the waterfront at Foro Umberto 1—try the Riso di Paradise, a concoction of chocolate, rice, and whipped cream, and you'll come back daily (closed in winter).

Antica Focacceria San Francesco ★ SICILIAN/SNACKS   Palermo street fare is good anywhere you have it, but it's especially savory in the atmospheric, marble-floored surroundings of this institution founded in 1834. If you've shied away from buying a *panino con la milza* (a bread roll stuffed with slices of boiled spleen and melted cheese) from a street vendor, you might want to jump in and try this delicious specialty here. You can also snack or lunch on *panelle* (deep-fried chickpea fritters), *ararancini di riso* (rice balls stuffed with tomatoes and peas or mozzarella), *focaccia farcita* (flat pizza baked with various fillings), or a

Antica Focacceria San Francesco.

number of other sandwiches, curtly dispensed from a busy counter.

Via A. Paternostro 58. www.afsf.it. ℰ **091-320264.** Sandwiches 3€–5€. Daily 11am–11pm (closed Tues Oct–Mar). Bus: 103, 105, or 225.

Casa del Brodo ★ SICILIAN With a setting in two plain rooms on the edge of the now sadly diminished Vucciria market, this century-old institution serves old Sicilian specialties that you might not encounter outside of home kitchens. *Fritelle di fava* (fava beans) are fried with vegetables and cheese; *carni bollite* (boiled meats) is a tantalizing assortment of tender, herb-flavored meats; and the *macco di fave* (meatballs and tripe) is a carnivore's delight. The namesake *brodo* (broth) is served several different ways, best as tortellini in brodo, with house-made pasta. If in doubt, order one of the fixed-price menus.

Corso Vittorio Emanuele 175. www.casadelbrodo.it. ℰ **091-321655.** Main courses 8€–16€; fixed-price menus from 20€. Wed–Mon 12:30–3pm and 7:30–11pm (closed Sun June–Sept). Bus: 103, 104, 105, 118, or 225.

Ferro di Cavallo ★ SICILIAN Bright red walls seem to rev up the energy to high levels in this ever-busy favorite, but the buzz is really about the good, plain food served at very reasonable prices. There's a menu, and a decent *antipasti* platter offers a nice sampling of *panelle* (fried chickpea fritters) and other street food, but go with the daily specials to get the full flavor of the kitchen. The preference is for beans and celery, broad beans and vegetables, meatballs in tomato sauce, boiled veal, and other classics. Service hovers between nonchalant and brusque, but the jovial atmosphere compensates, and you'll pay very little for your homey meal.

Via Venezia 20. www.ferrodicavallopalermo.it. © **091-331835.** Main courses 7€. Mon–Sat 10am–3:30pm and 7:45–11:30pm. Bus: 103, 104, 105, 118, or 225.

Ottava Nota ★★ SICILIAN "New Sicilian" is in full force at the most exciting of the restaurants that have opened in the once derelict Kalsa district in recent years, where the sleek surroundings are the setting for creative takes on Sicilian classics. Tuna tartare is served with avocado, risotto is laced with leeks and tuna caviar, and eggplant meatballs are topped with tomato cream. Duck, beef, and fish are market fresh and beautifully prepared, but you may not want to go beyond the pastas with fresh seafood—linguine with scallops, risotto with shrimp, tagliatelle with sea urchins. Service is strictly

The magnificent Teatro Massimo.

old-school—friendly and attentive—and a meal usually begins with a complimentary glass of prosecco.

Via Butera 55. ℂ **091-6168601.** Main courses 10€–20€. Mon 8–11pm, Tues–Sun 12:30–3:30pm and 8–11pm. Bus: 103, 104, 105, 118, or 225.

Entertainment & Nightlife

Palermo is a cultural center of some note, with an opera and ballet season running from November to July. The principal venue for cultural presentations is the restored **Teatro Massimo ★★**, Piazza G. Verdi (www.teatromassimo.it; ℂ **091-6053111**), which boasts the third largest indoor stage in Europe. Francis Ford Coppola shot the climactic opera scene here for *The Godfather: Part III*. Built between 1875 and 1897 in a neoclassical style, the theater was restored in 1997 to celebrate its 100th birthday. Ticket prices range from 10€ to 125€. The box office is open Tuesday to Sunday 10am to 3pm. ***Note:*** The Teatro Massimo can be visited Tuesday through Sunday from 10am to 3pm. Visits cost 5€. Guided tours in English are given Tuesday through Saturday from 10am to 3pm (bus: 101, 102, 103, 104, 107, 122, or 225).

Side Trips from Palermo

For Palermitans, a warm summer day means one thing—a trip to **Mondello Lido,** 12km (7½ miles) west of Palermo, where Belle Epoque Europeans once came to winter. Their Art Nouveau villas face a sandy beach that stretches for about 2km (1¼ miles), though there's little or no elbow room in July and August. Bus no. 806 makes the 15-minute trip to Mondello from Piazza Sturzo behind the Teatro Politeama.

Should you wish to do more than lie on a beach, many other sights are within easy reach of Palermo. The tour below are our best picks.

MONREALE ★★★
10km (6 miles) S of Palermo

On the Mons Regalis overlooking the Conca d'Oro (the Golden Valley), this hilltop village would be just another of the many that dot this fertile area south of Palermo if it weren't for its majestic Duomo, one of Italy's greatest medieval treasures, carpeted in shimmering mosaics. The locals even have a saying, "To come to Palermo without having seen Monreale is like coming in like a donkey and leaving like an ass."

GETTING THERE   The **AST bus** (www.aziendasiciliana trasporti.it; ℂ **840-000323**) leaves about every hour or so throughout the day from Palermo's Piazza Giulio Cesare (Central Train station) and Piazza Indipendenza (2.10€ one-way). If you are **driving** (it's about a 30-minute drive), leave your vehicle at the municipal car park at Via Ignazio Florio. From there you can take a cab or walk up the 99 steps that lead to the cathedral.

Exploring the Duomo
Duomo ★★ CATHEDRAL   Legend has it that William II had the idea of this cathedral in a dream when, during a hunting expedition, he fell asleep under a carob tree. While slumbering, the Virgin Mary appeared to him, indicating where a treasure chest was located—and with this loot he was to build a church in her honor. Legends aside, William's ambition to leave his mark was the force behind the last— and the greatest—of Sicily's Arab-Norman cathedrals with Byzantine interiors. Best of all, the cathedral in

Monreale never underwent any of the "improvements" that were applied to the cathedral of Palermo, and therefore its original beauty was preserved.

For the most part, the exterior of the building is nothing remarkable. But inside, mosaics comprise some 130 individual scenes, depicting biblical and religious events, covering some 6,400 sq. m (68,889 sq. ft.), and utilizing some 2,200 kg (4,850 lb.) of gold. The shop in the arcade outside the entrance sells a detailed plan of the mosaics with a legend detailing what's what, a mandatory aid to enjoying the spectacle; binoculars are also handy.

Episodes from the Old Testament are depicted in the central nave (a particularly charming scene shows Noah's Ark riding the waves) while the side aisles illustrate scenes from the New Testament. Christ

The cathedral of Monreale.

Pantocrator, the Great Ruler, looks over it all from the central apse; actually, he gazes off to one side, toward scenes from his life. Just below is a mosaic of the Teokotos (Mother of God) with the Christ child on her lap, bathed in light from the small window above the main entrance. Among the angels and saints flanking Teokotos is Thomas à Becket, the Archbishop of Canterbury who was murdered on the orders of William's father-in-law, Henry II (this is one of the earliest portraits of the saint; he is the second from the right).

William II is buried here, and also honored with a mosaic showing him being crowned by Christ. The heart of St. Louis, or Louis IX, a 13th-century king of France, rests in the urn in which it was placed when the king died during a crusade in Tunisia; the urn was transported to Sicily, then ruled by Louis's younger brother, Charles of Anjou.

The lovely cloisters adjacent to the cathedral are an Arabesque fantasy, surrounded by 228 columns topped with capitals carved with scenes from Sicily's Norman history. A splendid fountain in the shape of a palm tree adds to the romance of the place.

Piazza Guglielmo il Buono. ℂ **091-6404413.** Free admission to the cathedral; 2€ north transept and treasury; 2€ roof; 8€ cloisters, 4€ ages 18–25, free for children 17 and under and EU citizens 65 and over. Mon–Sat 8am–1pm and 2:30–6:30pm, Sun 8am–1pm; Cloisters: daily 9am–7pm.

CEFALÙ ★★

81km (50 miles) E of Palermo

The former fishing village of Cefalù, anchored between the sea and a craggy limestone promontory, has grown into a popular resort, though it will never be a rival to Taormina. If you saw the Oscar-winning film *Cinema Paradiso,* you've already been charmed by the town,

The Old Town of Cefalù.

though the filmmakers wisely left out the hordes of white-fleshed northern Europeans who roast themselves on the crescent-shaped **beach,** one of the best along the northern coast. Towering 278m (912 ft.) above the beach and town is **La Rocca,** a massive and much-photographed crag. The Greeks thought it evoked a head, so they named the village Kephalos, which in time became Cefalù. It's a long, hot, sweaty climb up to the top, but once there, the view is panoramic, extending all the way to the skyline of Palermo in the west or to Capo d'Orlando in the east.

GETTING THERE   From Palermo, some three dozen **trains** (www.trenitalia.com; ☏ **892021**) head east to Cefalù (trip time: 1 hr.). Trains pull into the Stazione

Termini, Piazza Stazione (✆ **892021**). **SAIS buses** (✆ **091-6171141**) run between Palermo and Cefalù.

By **car,** follow Route 113 east from Palermo to Cefalù; count on at least 1½ hours of driving time (longer if traffic is bad). Once in Cefalù, park along either side of Via Roma for free, or pay 1€ per hour for a spot within one of the two lots signposted from the main street; both are within an easy walk of the town's medieval core.

VISITOR INFORMATION   The **Cefalù Tourist Office,** Corso Ruggero 77 (✆ **0921-421050**), is open Monday to Saturday 8am to 7:30pm, Sunday 9am to 1pm. Closed on Sunday in winter.

Exploring Cefalù

Getting around Cefalù on foot is easy—no cars are allowed in the historic core. The city's main street is **Corso Ruggero,** which starts at Piazza Garibaldi, site of one of a quartet of gateways to the town.

Duomo ★★★ CHURCH   Anchored on a wide square at the foot of towering La Rocca, the twin-towered facade of the duomo forms a landmark visible for miles around. Legend has it that Roger II ordered this mighty church to be constructed in the 12th century after his life was spared in a violent storm off the coast. In reality, he probably built it to flex his muscle with the papacy and show the extent of his power in Sicily. Inside are more mosaics, and even if you've become inured to the charms of these shimmering scenes in Palermo and Monreale, you're in for a bit of a surprise: This being a Norman church, Christ is depicted as a blond, not a brunette. In his hand is a Bible, a standard accessory in these images of Christ the Pantocrator (the Ruler), with the verse, "I am the light of the

world; he who follows me shall not walk in darkness."
Columns in the nave are said to be from the much-ruined Temple of Diana halfway up La Rocca (you'll stop to inspect the rest of the stony remains if you make the climb to the top).

Piazza del Duomo. © **0921-922021.** Free admission. Summer daily 8am–noon and 3:30–7pm; off season daily 8am–noon and 3:30–5pm.

Museo Mandralisca MUSEUM   There is only one reason to step into this small museum, and it's a compelling one: "Ritratto di un Uomo Ignoto" ("Portrait of an Unknown Man"), a 1470 work by the Sicilian painter Antonello da Messina. Seeing this young man with a sly smile and twinkling eyes—some scholars say he was a pirate from the island of Lipari—is an experience akin to seeing the "Mona Lisa," and you won't have to fight your way through camera-wielding crowds to do so.

Via Mandralisca 13. © **0921-421547.** Admission 5€. Daily 9am–1pm and 3–7pm.

Where to Eat

For cakes and cookies, stop by **Pasticceria Serio Pietro,** V. G. Giglio 29 (© **0921-422293**), which also sells more than a dozen flavors of the most delicious gelato in town.

Osteria del Duomo ★★ SICILIAN/SEAFOOD
A prime spot across from the duomo with great views of the Rocca alone would make this a worthy stop, and the fresh seafood does justice to the locale. Seafood salads are a perfect choice for lunch on a summer's day, and piscivores will love the *carpaccio de pesce* (raw, thinly sliced fish). Carnivores can tuck into the

similarly excellent carpaccio of beef. Try to reserve ahead on weekends.

Via Seminario 3. ℓ **0921-421838.** Main courses 8€–16€. Tues–Sun noon–midnight. Closed mid-Nov to mid-Dec.

SEGESTA ★★★

75km (47 miles) SW of Palermo

The **Tempio di Segesta**, one of the best-preserved ancient Doric temples in all of Italy, proves yet again that the Greeks had a remarkable eye for where to build. Part of the ruined ancient city of Segesta, for millennia this beautiful structure in a lonely field overlooking the sea has been delighting those lucky enough to set eyes upon it. The temple was especially popular with 18th-century artists traveling in Sicily, whose paintings usually included herds of sheep and cattle in or surrounding the temple.

GETTING THERE   From Palermo, three trains a day make the 1¾- to 2-hour journey. The station is about a 1km (½-mile) walk to the park entrance. It's more convenient to reach Segesta **by bus; Tarantola** (ℓ **0924-31020**) operates four buses from Piazza Giulio Cesare (Central Train Station) in Palermo (journey time: 1¾ hour).

By **car,** take the autostrada (A29) running between Palermo and Trapani. The exit at Segesta is clearly marked. The journey takes a little under an hour from Palermo.

Exploring the Parco Archaeologico (The Archaeological Park)

The archaeological site, which is outside the modern town of Calatafimi, is still the subject of study by archaeologists from around the world. There's a small, canopied eating area opposite the only cafe, where visitors can unwind or rest during their visit.

Parco Archaeologico Segesta ★★★ RUINS
The **Tempio di Segesta (Temple of Segesta)** stands on a 304m (997-ft.) hill, on the edge of a deep ravine carved by the Pispisa River. Built in the 5th century B.C., it was never finished; the columns were never fluted and the roof was never placed on top. This, of course, does not affect the temple's greatest assets: the view down the hillside to the sea and the views of the temple from afar. Segesta's other great sight is the perfectly preserved **Teatro (Theater),** hewn out of rock at the top of 431m (1,414 ft.) Mount Barbaro (it's accessible by a hike of 4km [2½ miles] or by buses that run every half hour, cost 1.50€). The *cavea* of 20 semicircular rows could seat 4,000 spectators, who enjoyed views across the surrounding farmland to the Gulf of Castellamare. Those stunning views surely competed with any performance—and still do, during summertime stagings of operas, concerts, and plays.

Parco Archaelogico Segesta. ℂ **0924-952356**. Combined ticket with Parco Archeologico in Selinunte (p. 632), valid for 3 days: 9€ adults, 4.50€ ages 18–25, free children 17 and under. Mar daily 9am–6pm, Apr–Sept daily 8:30am–7pm, Oct–Feb daily 9am–5pm. Ticket office closes 1 hr before park closes.

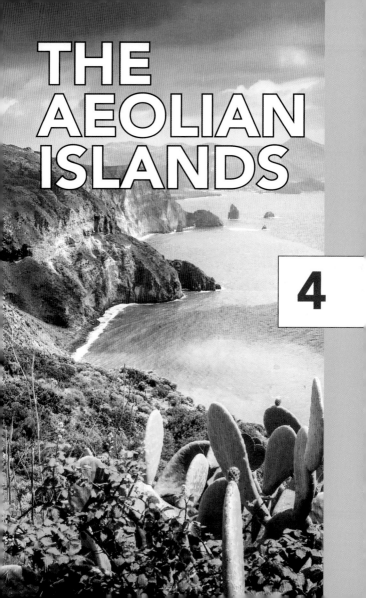

THE
AEOLIAN
ISLANDS

4

Threhe Aeolian Islands can seem like exotic getaways, as close as they are to Sicily's civilized north coast. Though the seven islands share sparkling waters and lava-etched landscapes, they vary widely. **Lipari** is the largest and most densely populated, while **Stromboli** is the most distant and the most volcanically active. **Vulcano,** with its sulfur-rich mud baths, is the closest to the rest of Sicily. **Panarea** is the smallest, and **Salina** produces the best wine. **Filicudi** and **Alicudi** are the wildest.

They are all sought-after summer retreats. The islands are still relatively quiet in May and June and become so again in September. They are also a scenic delight off-season, though many businesses close for the season at the end of September and don't reopen until May. Whenever you come, expect a breeze. This is where Aeolus, god of the winds, dwelled, and when the winds kick up in the afternoon, it's easy to imagine why.

GETTING THERE   **Ferries** and **hydrofoils** service all the Aeolian Islands from the port of **Milazzo,** 40km (25 miles) west of Messina. Hydrofoils are faster than ferries, getting you to Vulcano in an hour (ferries take twice as long), yet ferries are roomier, and allow you to stay out on the deck on your way there. **Ustica Lines,**

PREVIOUS PAGE: **View of Vulcano island from Lipari island.**

Via Rizzo (www.usticalines.it; ✆ **090-928-7821**) operates numerous daily ferry and hydrofoil routes to all islands, as well as seasonal routes from the mainland at Reggio Calabria. From July to September, it's possible to book hydrofoil tickets on Ustica Lines directly from Naples to Stromboli. **N.G.I.,** Via dei Mille 26 (www.ngi-spa.it; ✆ **800-250-000** toll free from Italy or 090-928-4091) runs ferry services to certain islands. From Naples, **SNAV** (www.snav.it; ✆ **081-4285555**) operates a seasonal service (late May to early Sept) to all the islands except Filicudi and Alicudi. Note that all ferry services charge a 1€ fee per person for entry to the islands. In the event of a storm or inclement weather, service can be halted for days.

Milazzo is served by frequent **train service** (www.trenitalia.it; ✆ **892-021;** from Messina and Palermo. From the station, take the shuttle bus that drops you off at the port (1€), or take a taxi, which will cost you around 10€. **Giuntabus** (www.giuntabus.com; ✆ **090-673782**) runs buses approximately every hour from Messina on weekdays with some going all the way to the port. If you're **driving** from Messina or Palermo, take the A20 autostrada until you come to the turnoff for the port at Milazzo, and follow the directions for *"garage/imbarchi,"* where you can also park your car safely.

VULCANO ★★★

25km (15 miles) NW of Milazzo

The ancients thought Vulcano was the home of Vulcan, the god of fire, and also a gateway to Hades. A climb to the to the rim of the active Gran Cratere (Big Crater), or Vulcano della Fosse, and a look inside the

The mud baths of Laghetti di Funghi in Vulcano.

sulfur-belching hole helps you understand how these legends came to be.

For centuries, the island remained uninhabited out of fear of the volcano. Today, however, Vulcano is a stamping ground of wealthy Italians who've built villas and partake in a summertime party culture. Even so, the big attraction is down to earth: Vulcano's thermal baths, known for their curative powers, are said to be especially helpful in relieving rheumatic suffering. Vulcano also has the best beaches in the Aeolians, if you don't find the black volcanic sands to be off-putting.

Vulcano is the island closest to the Sicilian mainland, and ferries and hydrofoils stop here before going on to the other islands. If the wind is blowing in the right direction, you'll get a good whiff of the island's sulfurous fumes before pulling into port.

ESSENTIALS

GETTING AROUND   Most people walk, but a private company, **Scaffidi** (*©* **090-9853017**), runs **buses**

from the port area to Piano, a village in the southwestern interior of the island, and to Gelso at the southern tip. Seven buses operate Monday through Saturday; two on Sunday. If you'd rather rent a bike or scooter, go to **Da Paolo,** Via Porto Levante (© **090-9852112**), open May through November daily from 8am to 8:30pm.

WHAT TO SEE & DO

The island's fabled mud baths, **Laghetti di Fanghi,** are off the docks along Via Provinciale. A 56m-high (184-ft.) *faraglione,* or "stack" is a massive pit of thick, sulfurous gunk that is said to greatly relieve certain skin diseases and rheumatism suffering. The mud discolors everything, so in summer expect to find the muddy pools brimming with naked tourists. (Soothing as a soak is, and it's an island experience not to miss, it's best not to linger more than half an hour or so, as the waters are radioactive.) Mud bathers wash off the gunk in hot springs nearby. The baths are open from Easter to October, daily from 6:30am to 8pm; admission is 1€.

After a soak, head to the dramatic **Spiaggia Sabbie Nere (Black Sands Beach),** the finest in the archipelago. It stretches from Porto di Levante to Porto di Ponente and is a 20-minute walk north from the mud baths along Via Ponente.

Take time off from the beach to follow the only road north to **Vulcanello,** at the island's northern tip. A small cone erupted in 183 B.C., spiking its way up through the earth to become a permanent fixture on the landscape. The toy-like volcano erupted again in 1888, creating what the islanders call a *Valle dei Mostri* (Valley of Monsters) of bizarrely shaped lava fountains.

The view from Vulcano's famed Gran Cratere.

The Gran Cratere ★★★

To the south of Porto di Levante lies one of the greatest attractions in the Aeolians, the Gran Cratere. You can get to the crater only by a fairly easy hike, about a 3-hour round trip on a marked trail. The route is not shaded, so go early in the morning or late in the day; load up on sunscreen and water; and wear sturdy hiking shoes. Your reward will be dramatic views of some of the other Aeolian Islands and, of course, a looking into the 450m (1,476 ft.) crater. Steaming vapors emissions still spew from the crater, discouraging you from lingering for too long.

WHERE TO STAY & EAT

Les Sables Noirs ★★ Vulcano's most luxurious outpost overlooks a black-sand beach. While stucco and bamboo suggest a Caribbean resort, the guest rooms and apartments opening to a wide balcony or to patios surrounding the pool are decidedly Mediterranean in style, with tile floors and pastel hues. Guests have use of a private section of the beach out front.

Via Porto di Ponente. www.framonhotels.com. ℭ **090-9850.** 43 units. 230€–290€ double. Closed Oct–Mar. **Amenities:** Restaurant; 2 bars; outdoor pool; Wi-Fi (free).

Vincenzino ★ AEOLIAN/SICILIAN   A large, plain room near the port is the setting for hefty portions of good island fare. Fish is locally caught and expertly grilled, and pastas are laden with fresh seafood— *risotto alla pescatora,* with crayfish, mussels, and other seafood and an island classic, pasta with fresh sardines.

Via Porto di Levante. www.ristorantevincenzino.com. ℗ **090-9852016.** Main courses 8€–10€. Daily noon–3pm and 7–10pm.

LIPARI ★★

5km (3 miles) N of Vulcano, 30km (19 miles) N of Milazzo

Known to Greeks as *Meligunis,* Lipari is the largest of the islands (36 sq km/14 sq miles) and it's the best base for exploring the archipelago. Lipari town sits on a plateau of red volcanic rock on the southeastern shore, framed by two ports: **Marina Lunga,** where the larger vessels dock, and **Marina Corta,** the smaller fishermen's harbor. There are four other villages on the island. As you circumnavigate the terrain, you'll notice barren fields locals call *Rocce Rosse,* or the "red rocks." These yield pumice, used in everything from toothpaste to face creams, and the powder is big business on the island.

ESSENTIALS

GETTING AROUND   Large **boats** dock at the deepwater port of **Marina Lunga,** while the smaller vessels call in at **Marina Corta.** Most of the city life lies between these two ports and its side streets, so if you need anything once you disembark, it's all nearby. **Taxis** are found at the port ready to whisk you to wherever you need to go; to pre-book service, call one of the local drivers at ℗ **338-525603**. Most hotels offer courtesy shuttle-services to and from the port;

check to see if the one you're staying at provides a transfer service.

Lipari is serviced by a **bus** network, run by **Guglielmo Urso** (www.ursobus.it; ✆ **090-981-1026**). Buses leave from Marina Lunga about every hour (more frequently in summer), stopping at various points around the island. No point on the island is less than a half-hour ride away. A bus schedule is provided by the tourist office and at the website. Tickets can be bought at the ticket kiosk at the port or purchased on board from the driver, at no extra charge, for 2€.

To get around on your own (cars are not allowed on the island during the summer), a cheap, efficient option is to **rent a bike** (average rates 10€ per day) or **motor scooter** (20€ daily, not including fuel, but including the safety helmet). A security deposit (cash or credit card) is required, together with identification. Two rental outlets are **Da Marcello,** Via Sottomonastero, Marina Lunga (✆ **090-9811234**); and **Da Tullio,** Via Amendola 22, Marina Lunga (✆ **090-9880540**). To rent a small car, try **Aveden** (www.aveden.it; ✆ **090-9811026;** Via dei Cappuccini.

VISITOR INFORMATION   The **tourist office** in Lipari is at Via Vittorio Emanuele 202 (✆ **090-9880095**). In July and August, it is open Monday to Friday 8:30am to 2pm and 4:30 to 7:30pm, Saturday 8am to 2pm. From September to June, hours are Monday to Friday 8:30am to 2pm and 4:30 to 7:30pm.

WHAT TO SEE & DO

Lipari Town huddles beneath a volcanic-rock crag that has served as a natural fortress throughout the millennia. It sheltered the acropolis of the Greek *Lipara* then a castle, with thick walls that were refortified as late as the 1700s. Within them is a full-fledged town: churches, the former bishop's palace, a few old homes, and on the highest point, the 15th-century Duomo (cathedral).

In the Lower Town, the remains of Greek walls dating from the 5th and 4th centuries B.C., the Roman gate, and altar dedicated to the cult of Demeter litter a neglected patch behind a fence visible off Via Marconi.

Museo Archeologico Luigi Bernabo' Brea ★★★

The 17th-century Palazzo Vescovile, or bishop's palace, and other pavilions house an admirable collection of finds from the islands and Sicilian coast. Some of the glossy red ceramics, known as the "Diana style," date to 3000 B.C., while blades fashioned from obsidian, glass-like black volcanic rock, predate the use of metal in the ancient world. In burial urns from the 11th century B.C., Lipari islanders are buried in large jars with their bodies in fetal positions. A collection of theatrical masks, with some notably gruesome grins and leers, was unearthed in tombs from the 4th century to the 3rd century B.C.

Via del Castello. ℂ **090-9880174.** Admission 6€ adults, 3€ for ages 18–25, free for children 17. Daily 9am–1:30pm and 3–6pm (4–7pm May–Sept), Sun/holidays 9am–1:30pm.

Around the Island

The most popular spot on the island outside Lipari Town is the village of **Canneto,** 2km (1¼ miles) north on the east coast. Some of the best, most accessible beaches are here, including **Spiaggia Bianca,** named for the supposedly white sand, though it's really in hues of gray. In fact, most of the island's beaches are black volcanic sand or rock.

Mount Pilato, at 476m (1,562 ft.), is the ancient crater of a volcano that last erupted in A.D. 700. Fields around this crater are the source of raw material for

The beach in Canneto.

the island's pumice industry, and you'll walk through the fields of red stone along the path to the summit. For the best views on Lipari, head west of Lipari town about 4km (2½ miles) to **Quattrocchi** ("four eyes"), where you can make the steep climb to Quattrocchi Belvedere for a panoramic vistas over the entire archipelago.

WHERE TO STAY & DINE

Gattopardo Park Hotel ★★ An 18th-century villa surrounded by white bungalows exudes Aeolian style, with outdoor lounges and a breezy terraced dining room and bar. Simple but attractive guest quarters have tiled floors, wood-beamed ceilings, and terraces that open to lush gardens. Aside from the pool, swimming is from rocks in a nearby bay, and a free shuttle whisks guests to and from beaches around the island. Vico Diana. www.gattopardoparkhotel.it. © **090-9811035.** 60 units. 130€–220€ double. Rates include breakfast. Closed Nov–Feb. **Amenities:** Restaurant; bar; outdoor pool; room service; Wi-Fi (free).

The staff of Filippino restaurant.

Filippino ★★ SICILIAN/AEOLIAN This Aeolian institution is more than a century old and serves local specialties in two old-fashioned dining rooms and on a terrace filled with flowering shrubs. Age-old island preparations include risotto with squid ink and baby shrimp and swordfish with oranges and figs.

Piazza Mazzini. www.filippino.it. ℂ **090-9811002.** Reservations required July–Aug. Main courses 8€–15€. Daily noon–2:30pm and 7:30–10:30pm. Closed Nov 10–Dec 26.

Villa Meligunis ★ A compound of 17th-century fishermen's cottages suggests what life on the island one was, and still is for some, but here it's all about living well. A rooftop pool and terrace is a breezy private retreat, while guest rooms—the best with balconies and sea views—are simply furnished with wrought-iron bedsteads and other handsome pieces.

Via Marte 7. www.villameligunis.it. ℂ **090-9812426.** 32 units. 170€–225€ double. Rates include continental breakfast. **Amenities:** Restaurant; 2 bars; outdoor pool; room service; Wi-Fi (free).

STROMBOLI ★★★

30km (19 miles) N of Lipari, 63km (40 miles) N of Milazzo.

The big attraction on the easternmost Aeolian is its volcano, whose single cone measures 926m (3,038 ft.) and still puts on a formidable show of might. From most parts of the island you'll see the sluggish but still-active volcano puffing a bit of smoke. But a guided nighttime tour up the slopes reveals the real spectacle, the sight of lava glowing red-hot as it tumbles down to meet the sea with a loud hiss.

Human fireworks put Stromboli on the map in 1950, with the release of the Roberto Rossellini *cinéma vérité* film *Stromboli,* starring Ingrid Bergman. The love affair between married Bergman and Rossellini generated far more interest than the film did and temporarily put the skids on Bergman's American film career.

ESSENTIALS

GETTING AROUND   Sabbia Nera, Via Marina (www.sabbianerastromboli.com; ✆ 090-986390) books boat trips around Stromboli, calling at Ginostra and Strombolicchio. Trips last 3 hours and cost 20€ per person. Trips at night to see Sciara del Fuoco (see below) last 2 hours and cost 25€ per person. Most of these excursions leave from the beach at Ficogrande.

EXPLORING THE ISLAND

The island has two settlements. **Ginostra,** on the southwestern shore, is little more than a cluster of summer homes. **Stromboli,** on the northeastern shore, is a pleasantly scrappy little settlement strung along a black-sand beach.

Seeing the lava flow is the top reason to go to Stromboli.

The big attraction, of course, is the volcano. By law, the cone, **Gran Cratere**, can be visited only with a guide. Guide Alpine Autorizzate (© **090-986-211**) charges 20€ per person and leads groups on the 3-hour one-way trip up the mountain, leaving at 5pm and returning at 11pm. (The trip down takes only 2 hours, but you're allowed an hour at the rim.) About halfway up is a view of the **Sciara del Fuoco (Slope of Fire),** where lava glows red-hot on its way down to meet the sea with a loud hiss. You can also make the ascent during the day, but the views of the lava slopes are far less dramatic by day.

Otherwise, there isn't much to see on Stromboli. Film buffs can follow Via Vittorio Emanuele to the see the outside of the little pink house where Ingrid Bergman and Roberto Rossellini "lived in sin" during the filming of *Stromboli*. On the northeast coast is **Strombolicchio,** a steep basalt block measuring 43m (141 ft.) high that you can climb on ste2ps hewn out of rock. Once at the top, you'll be rewarded with a panoramic view of the Aeolians, and on a clear day you can see as far as Calabria on the Italian mainland.

WHERE TO STAY & EAT

La Sirenetta Park Hotel ★★ A scenic terrace, a beautiful swimming pool, and a beach out front are all excellent places to while away a day while waiting to make a nighttime ascent up the volcano. Airy, tile-floored guest rooms are comfortable but do service to the island with attractively simple style. The excellent dining room ensures you won't have to venture far for a meal, and a dive center offers water-skiing, sailing, and windsurfing.

Via Marina 33. www.lasirenetta.it. © **090-986025.** 60 units. 120€–300€ double. Rates include breakfast. Closed Nov 1 to mid-Mar. **Amenities:** Restaurant; 2 bars; saltwater outdoor pool; tennis court; fitness center; room service; water sports; Wi-Fi (free in some areas).

Punta Lena ★★ SICILIAN/AEOLIAN An old Aeolian house with a seaside terrace is a perfect setting for a simple island meal. The menu will offer what's been caught that day as well as some local-favorite pastas, including spaghetti *alla stromboliana* (with wild fennel, cherry tomatoes and breadcrumbs) and *gnocchi alla Saracena,* with whitefish, capers, olives, and tomatoes.

Via Marina 8 (Località Ficogrande). © **090-986204.** Reservations recommended. Main courses 8€–16€. Daily noon–2:30pm and 7–11pm. Closed Nov–Mar.

PANAREA

The smallest of the Aeolian archipelago is a jagged landscape surrounded by cobalt waters. Panarea has been inhabited since Neolithic times, and these days is especially popular with a wealthy few who retreat to beautiful villas on the island. Zimmari beach is the best place to dive into the inviting sea.

WHERE TO STAY & DINE

Hotel Quartara   A former grocery store that once rented basic rooms is now an idyllic island retreat, with bright-white guest quarters that are floored in hand-painted ceramic tiles and filled with Sicilian handicrafts; all have terraces. Beaches, like everything else on the tiny island, are a short walk away, and the pool is a beautiful, isolated hideaway. The indoor/outdoor restaurant the best on the island.

Via S. Pietro 15. www.quartarahotel.com. ℭ **090-983027.** 13 units. 200€–350€ double. Rates include breakfast. Closed Nov–Mar. **Amenities:** Restaurant; bar; outdoor pool; Jacuzzi; Wi-Fi (free).

SALINA

The name Salina means salt and comes from the salt lake near the village of Marina di Salina. The island also famous produces grapes that are made into Malvasia, the sweet dessert wine. The capers produced on the island are celebrated at the Caper Festival (*Sagra del Cappero*) in the first week of June. One of the best beaches in the Aeolians is the one at Pollara.

WHERE TO STAY & DINE

Capofaro ★★★   Though the beautiful surroundings are in keeping with the island aesthetic, there's nothing plain or simple about the enticing guest rooms etched out of several homes in a vineyard near the lighthouse. Spacious, minimalist quarters blend island traditions and contemporary chic, and each has a private balcony and/or terrace. The in-house restaurant serves simple Aeolian classics.

Via Faro 3. www.capofaro.it. ℗ **090-9844330.** 20 units. 150€–260€. Rates include breakfast. **Amenities:** Restaurant; bar; outdoor pool; Wi-Fi (free).

FILICUDI & ALICUDI

Quaint **Filicudi** attracts vacationers looking to forgo the crowds in favor of unspoilt surroundings. Three villages are home to a couple of hundred villagers and the basalt coastlines plunge dramatically into the sea below. Cliffs give way to rocky beaches in a few places, such as Le Punte, near the port. Much of the land is protected as a nature preserve, with trails crossing the rugged landscapes to a few landmarks that include a village of 4,000-year-old stone huts near Capo Graziano. Just offshore, the spire-like La Canna, a tall, narrow volcanic rock, shoots dramatically out of the sea.

The most westerly of the islands, **Alicudi,** is also the most removed from civilization—there are no paved roads, the pace is slow, and donkeys might outnumber the hundred or so islanders. Isolation and rugged charm are, in fact, the main draws of the island. There's not much to do other than soak in the atmosphere, swim from the rocks, and make the fairly strenuous climb through terraced fields to the crater atop Monte Fillo dell'Arpa. A few islanders take in guests and make meals for their visitors.

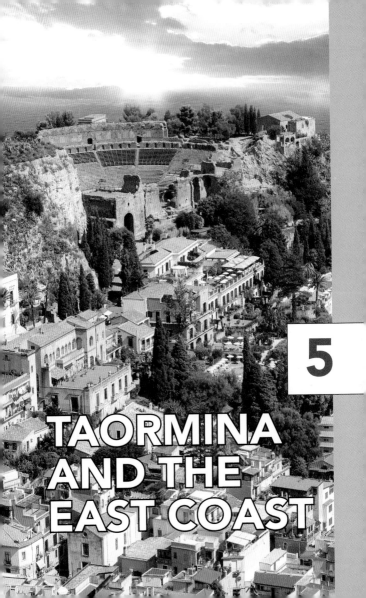

5

TAORMINA AND THE EAST COAST

t would be easy to stay put in Taormina, with its commanding views and privileged mountainside location. Sooner or later, though, the beaches will entice you down to the coast. Or, you might be tempted to make the ascent up Mount Etna, looming to the south.

TAORMINA ★★★

53km (33 miles) N of Catania, 53km (33 miles) S of Messina, 250km (155 miles) E of Palermo

Guy de Maupassant, the 19th-century French short-story writer, played the tourist shill and wrote, "Should you only have one day to spend in Sicily and you ask me 'what is there to see?' I would reply 'Taormina' without any hesitation. It is only a landscape but one in which you can find everything that seems to have been created to seduce the eyes, the mind and the imagination." Lots of visitors have felt the same way. The Roman poet Ovid loved Taormina, and 18th-century German man of letters Wolfgang Goethe put the town on the Grand Tour circuit when he extolled its virtues in his widely published diaries. Oscar Wilde was one of the gentlemen who made Taormina, as writer and dilettante Harold Acton put it, "a polite synonym for Sodom," and Greta Garbo is one of many film legends who have sought a bit of privacy here.

It could be said that with its beauty and sophistication Taormina has a surfeit of star quality itself. The town often seems more international than Sicilian and has so many admirers that visitors often outnumber

PREVIOUS PAGE: **A view of Taormina and its Greek amphitheater.**

locals. Then again, perched precariously on a steep cliff halfway between the sinister slopes of Mount Etna and the glittering Ionian Sea, its captivating alleyways lined with churches and *palazzi*, Taormina is almost over-the-top beautiful, and what could be more Sicilian than that?

ESSENTIALS

Getting There

By Air You can fly to Taormina from airports throughout Italy and the rest of Europe to Catania. The **Aeroporto di Catania,** aka Fontanarossa (www.aeroporto. catania.it; ✆ **095-7239111**) is about an hour from Taormina by taxi (about 60€) and well served by bus. From Fontanarossa, there are nine Taormina-bound buses per day, stopping in downtown Catania before heading up the coast to Taormina. Travel time by bus from Catania to Taormina is about 1½ hours; tickets are 5€ one-way. Full schedules are available from **Interbus** (www.etnatrasporti.it).

By Bus Taormina is well served by buses, from Palermo and other parts of Sicily, most of which connect through Catania (see Interbus, above). Taormina's bus station is on Via Pirandello, near Porta Messina, on the north end of town.

By Car If you're arriving by **car** from Messina, head south along A18 and follow the well-marked exits for Taormina. From Catania, take the A18 north, toward Messina. Exit the autostrada at the Taormina exit, which lies just north of a series of highway tunnels. If you're driving from the mainland, you'll cross the 5km-wide (3-miles) Stretto di Messina (Strait of Messina) by one of the regular car ferries between the Calabrian port of Villa San Giovanni (just north of Reggio

Calabria, essentially the "toe" of the Italian peninsula's boot shape) and Messina. From Messina, Taormina is 52km/32 miles south, about 45 min. Find out if your hotel has parking and if there's a fee, and get very clear instructions about how to arrive—Taormina is a mind-boggling maze of tiny one-way streets and hairpin turns. Otherwise, take advantage of the large public **parking garages** just outside the old town, both clearly sign-posted with blue *P*s on all roads that approach Taormina. On the north side of town, **Parking Lumbi** (✆ **0942-24345**) charges 14€ per day (16€ per day in Aug) and has a free shuttle from the garage to the Porta Messina gate of Taormina proper. On the south end of town, **Parking Porta Catania** (✆ **0942-620196**) is another multilevel garage with slightly higher rates than Lumbi (15€ per day, 17€ per day in Aug) but with the advantage of being practically in town (it's just 100m/328 ft. from the Porta Catania city gate). Down by the beach at Mazzarò, in the vicinity of the lower cable-car station, is **Parking Mazzarò** (14€ per day, 16€ in Aug).

By Train **Trains** from mainland Italy come down from Rome and Naples through Calabria and across the Strait of Messina to Sicily on ferries equipped with railroad tracks on the cargo deck. At Messina, the trains split, with part of the train going to Palermo and the part south along the east coast to Siracusa. Taormina is between 40 minutes and 1½ hours from Messina, depending on the speed of your train. The trip from Naples takes about 9 hrs.; nightly service is equipped with sleeping accommodations. See www.trenitalia. com for complete schedules. Keep in mind that Taormina's train station, which is shared with the seaside town of Giardini-Naxos, lies down the hill from town, 1.6km (1 mile) away. From the station, you have to

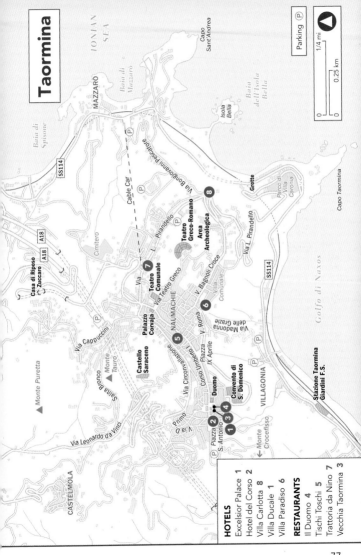

Taormina

HOTELS
Excelsior Palace 1
Hotel del Corso 2
Villa Carlotta 8
Villa Ducale 1
Villa Paradiso 6

RESTAURANTS
Il Duomo 4
Tischi Toschi 5
Trattoria da Nino 7
Vecchia Taormina 3

The resort town of Taormina.

take a bus up the hill to Taormina proper (9am–9pm, every 15–45 min.; 2€ one-way), or a taxi (about 15€).

Exploring Taormina

Just about everything to see in Taormina unfolds from the main pedestrian drag, **Corso Umberto I**, which slices through town from Porta Messina, in the north, to Porta Catania, in the south. It only takes about 10 minutes to walk the length of the Corso. Taormina is also a handy base for day trips to Mount Etna—the high-altitude visitor areas are only about 1 hour away by car.

Teatro Greco (Teatro Antico) ★★★ RUINS
With their penchant for building in beautiful settings, the Greeks perched the second-largest ancient theater in Sicily, after the one in Siracusa, on the rocky flanks of Mount Tauro. The backdrop of smoldering Mount Etna and the sea crashing far below certainly provided as much drama as any theatrical production. Romans rebuilt much of the theater, adding the finishing touches on what we see today in the 2nd century A.D., and put the arena to use for gladiatorial events. In ruin, but with much of the hillside *cavea*, or curved seating area, intact, the theater is still the setting for

performances and film screenings, greatly enhanced by columns and arches framing the sea and volcano in the background. Check with TaorminaArte's headquarters, Corso Umberto 19 (www.taoarte.it; © **0942-21142**), or at the tourist office for exact dates and show times.

Via del Teatro Greco. © **0942-21142.** Admission 8€. Apr–Sept daily 9am–7pm; Oct–Mar daily 9am–4pm.

Villa Comunale ★★★ PARK/GARDEN Of all the colorful characters who have spent time in Taormina, the one leaving the biggest mark may have been Lady Florence Trevelyan, who in the late 19th century created these beautiful gardens, now the city park also known as Parco Duca di Cesarò. Lady Trevelyan allegedly was asked to leave Britain after an entanglement with Edward, Prince of Wales, son of Queen Victoria. She settled in Taormina, married, and lived quite happily in the lovely, adjacent villa that is now the hotel Villa

A close up of Taormina's Greek Theater with Mount Etna in the distance.

MEET mighty MOUNT ETNA

Warning: Always get the latest report from the tourist office before setting out for a trip to Mount Etna. Adventurers have been killed by a surprise "belch" (volcanic explosion). Mount Etna remains one of the world's most active volcanoes, with sporadic gas, steam, lava, and ash emissions from its summit.

Looming menacingly over the coast of eastern Sicily, Mount Etna is the highest and largest active volcano in Europe. The peak changes in size over the years but it currently soars 3,324m (10,906 ft.). Etna has been active in modern times: In 1928, the little village of Mascali was buried under lava, and powerful eruptions in 1971, 1992, 2001, and 2003 caused extensive damage to facilities nearby. Throughout the year, episodes of spectacular but usually harmless lava

fountains, some hundreds of meters high, are not uncommon, providing a dramatic show for viewers in Taormina.

Etna has figured in history and in Greek mythology. Empedocles, the 5th-century B.C. Greek philosopher, is said to have jumped into its crater in the belief that he would be delivered directly to Mount Olympus to take his seat among the gods. It was under Etna that Zeus crushed the multiheaded, viper-riddled dragon Typhoeus, thereby securing domination over Olympus. Hephaestus, the god of fire and blacksmiths, made his headquarters in Etna, aided by the single-eyed Cyclops. The Greeks warned that when Typhoeus tried to break out of his prison, lava erupted and earthquakes cracked the land. That must mean that the monster nearly escaped on March 11,1669, one of

Paradiso (see p. 85). Her liaison with a farmer, much of it conducted amid these groves and terraces, supposedly inspired D.H. Lawrence's "Lady Chatterley's Lover." Lady Trevelyan built the stone and brick the most violent eruptions ever—it destroyed Catania, about 27km (17 miles) away.

Etna is easy to reach by car from Taormina. The fastest way is to take the E45 auto-strada south to the Acireale exit. From here, follow the brown Etna signs west to Nicolosi, passing through several smaller towns along the way. From Nicolosi, keep following the Etna signs up the hill toward **Rifugio Sapienza** (1,923m/6,307 ft.), the starting point for all expeditions to the crater. Here, there's a faux–Alpine hamlet with tourist shops and services, cheap and ample parking, as well as the base station of the **Funivia del Etna** cable car (www.funiviaetna.com; ✆ **095-914141;** daily 9am–4:30pm), which takes you to the Torre del Filosofo (Philosopher's Tower) station at 2,900m (9,514 ft.). You can also hike up to the station, but

it's a strenuous hike that takes about 5 hours. From there, to reach the authorized crater areas at about 3,000m (9,843 ft., as close to the summit as visitors are allowed), you'll climb into white, *Star Wars*-ish off-road vehicles that make the final ascent over a scrabbly terrain of ash and dead ladybugs (dead ladybugs are everywhere on Mount Etna). Conditions at the crater zone are thrilling, but the high winds, exposure, and potential sense of vertigo are not for the faint of heart.

The round-trip cost of going to the top of Etna, including the cable car ride, the off-road vans, and the requisite authorized guide at the crater zone, is about 55€. Etna is not a complicated excursion to do on your own, but if you'd prefer to go with a tour, Taormina is chock-full of agencies that organize Etna day trips.

pavilions in the park for bird watching and entertaining—it's too bad the gates are swung shut at sunset, because these fanciful follies would be perfect for whiling away a hot summer night. During the day, the

3 hectares (7½ acres) of beautifully groomed terraces provide a nice respite from the busy town, filled as they are with luxuriant Mediterranean vegetation, cobblestone walkways, picturesque stone stairways, and a sinuous path lining the park's eastern rim with superb views over the sea.

Via Bagnoli Croce. No phone. Free admission. Daily 8:30am–7pm (6pm in winter).

Where to Stay

The hotels in Taormina are the best in Sicily. All price ranges are available, with accommodations ranging from army cots to sumptuous suites.

If you're driving to a hotel at the top of Taormina, call ahead to see what arrangements can be made for your car. Ask for exact driving directions as well as instructions on where to park—the narrow, winding, one-way streets can be bewildering once you get here.

Excelsior Palace ★   Not a palace, really, but a sprawling pink grand hotel from the early 20th century that is conveniently tucked into one end of town just off Corso Umberto. Rooms here have not been upgraded since, well, since a time when burnt-orange bathroom tiles and floral carpets were all the rage. They're well maintained, though, and every one has a view—many of Mount Etna and the coastline—and many have little balconies with just enough room for two chairs. Though the place is often filled with groups, service is personal, attentive, and old-world, with waiters in ties and jackets serving cocktails in frumpy lounges full of overstuffed, slipcovered couches and armchairs. In the magnificent garden, many verdant acres are draped over a promontory high above the town and sea, the setting for a magnificently perched swimming pool—which in itself makes this a good summertime choice.

Via Toselli 8. www.excelsiorpalacetaormina.it. © **0942-23975.** 85 units. From 65€–125€ double. Rates include buffet breakfast. **Amenities:** Restaurant; bar; concierge; pool; Wi-Fi in public areas (free).

Hotel del Corso ★   You'll forgo spas, pools, and other chic luxuries in these fairly basic lodgings right in the heart of town, on Corso Umberto near the Duomo, but you won't give up views of the sea and Mount Etna. They fill the windows of many of the rooms and spread out below the top floor lounge, breakfast room, and sun terrace; some rooms have less dramatic but pleasing views of the town. Black-and-white terrazzo floors, iron bedsteads, and soothing neutral colors add a lot of spark to the comfortable guest rooms, a choice few of which have small balconies. Book well in advance, especially on weekends, when this good-value property fills up fast.

Corso Umberto 328. www.hoteldelcorsotaormina.com. © **0942-628698.** 15 units. 70€–110€ double. Rates include buffet breakfast. **Amenities:** Wi-Fi (free).

Villa Carlotta ★★★   This 1920s stone villa vaguely resembling a castle is an enchanting getaway at the edge of town—another creation of Andrea and Rosaria Quartucci, who work such magic at Villa Ducale (below). A wall of Byzantine catacombs adds an air of mystery, but what wins you over is the classic-yet-contemporary style and wonderful sense of privacy and comfort. Most of the warm-hued, stylish rooms have terraces and sea views, and many overlook the luxuriant rear gardens where a swimming pool is tucked into the greenery. As at Villa Ducale, service is personalized and attentive, and a shuttle bus makes a run down to the beach. Villa Carlotta also operates the sumptuous Taormina Luxury Apartments (www.taormina luxuryapartments.com), just up the street.

Via Pirandello 81. www.hotel villacarlottataormina.com. ℭ **0942-626058.** 23 units. 200€–350€ double. Closed Jan–early Mar. **Amenities:** Restaurant; concierge; health club; pool; Wi-Fi (free).

A bustling street in Taormina.

Villa Ducale ★★★ Andrea and Rosaria Quartucci have fashioned a family villa perched high on a hillside above the town into a warm and stylish getaway with flower-planted terraces, Mediterranenan gardens, and extraordinary eagle's-nest views that extend as far as Calabria. Distinctive rooms and suites, in the villa and a house across the road, are done in Sicilian chic, with stylish and extremely comfortable furnishings set against warm hues that play off terracotta floors; they are enlivened with beams, arches, and other architectural details, equipped with luxurious baths, and fitted out with fine linens and works by local artists. Service is exceedingly warm and personal, and a lavish buffet breakfast and complimentary sunset cocktails, accompanied by a spread of Sicilian appetizers, are served on a living room–like terrace; lunch and dinner are available on request. The hotel has no pool, but there's a Jacuzzi, and a shuttle makes a run to a private beach, and also to town.

Via Leonardo da Vinci 60. www.villaducale.com. ℭ **0942-28153.** 15 units. 240€–400€ double. Rates include buffet breakfast. Parking 10€. Closed Jan–early Mar. **Amenities:** Jacuzzi; room service; Wi-Fi (free).

Villa Paradiso ★★   Lady Florence Trevelyan, who created the beautiful gardens that are now the Villa Communale, lived in this villa until her death in 1907, and it passed to the Martorana family, three generations of whom have proven to be charming hoteliers. Family antiques, comfy armchairs and couches, and paintings (many presented by guests over the years) fill lounges and bright, handsomely decorated guest rooms, where balconies and sun-drenched sitting alcoves face the sea. Breakfast and dinners are served in a top-floor, glassed-in restaurant, Settimo Cielo (Seventh Heaven), which it really seemes to be. Between June and October, the hotel offers free shuttle service and free entrance to the Paradise Beach Club, about 6km (4 miles) to the east, in the seaside resort of Letojanni.

Via Roma 2. www.hotelvillaparadisotaormina.com. ☎ **0942-23921.** 37 units. 130€–210€ double. **Amenities:** Restaurant; bar; room service; Wi-Fi (fee).

Where to Eat

The ultimate Sicilian summer refreshment, the sorbet-like *granita,* is perfect at **Bam Bar,** not far from the Grand Hotel Timeo at Via di Giovanni 45 (☎ **0942-24355**). Specialties are the almond (*mandorla*) or white fig (*fico bianco),* but there are usually more than a dozen flavors to choose from.

Il Duomo ★★ SICILIAN   The decor leaves something to be desired, with harsh lighting and a green-and-orange color scheme—to avoid it, choose a table near the large window overlooking the Duomo, or better yet in good weather, on the side terrace. Fortunately, the food doesn't take any such liberties in taste and sticks to traditional Sicilian recipes, with some well-conceived modern twists. This is the best place in town to try pasta con sarde (with sardines and breadcrumbs); the fish is commendably fresh and nicely enlivened with capers, tomatoes, and olives.

Vico Ebrei. www.ristorantealduomo.it. *©* **0942-625656.** Main courses 10€–16€. Tues–Sun 12:30–3pm and 7:30–10:30pm.

Tischi Toschi ★★★ SICILIAN/SEAFOOD A

warm-hued yellow room facing a delightful little piazza and decorated with old ceramics is the setting for creative takes on old Sicilian classics. Even *pasta alla Norma* (with eggplant and ricotta) seems like a work of art here, and is thoughtfully topped with a grilled eggplant. Venture further, though, into some dishes you might not encounter in many other places—some top choices, if they're being served, are *insalata di pesce stocco*, a salad made from dried cod, raw fennel, and tomato dressed with olive oil and parsley, and *sarde a beccafico*, sardines stuffed with pine nuts and fennel and served with lemon and orange. Accompany anything with the delicious fried artichokes, and end a meal with the heavenly, refreshing lemon jelly.

Via F. Paladini 3. *©* **339-3642088.** Main courses 8€–18€. Daily noon–3pm and 6:30–11pm.

Trattoria da Nino ★ SICILIAN Good, no-

nonsense Sicilian *cucina casalinga* (home cooking) is the recipe for success in this unpretentious, brightly lit room (with an airy terrace in warm weather) across from the upper station of the cable car. Pastas are house-made (deliciously delicate gnocchi, little potato dumplings, are served *alla Norma,* with eggplant and ricotta), and the fish is fresh and served simply grilled. Nino's is a local institution, a 50-year veteran of the

Taormina dining scene, and it's always packed; they don't take reservations for groups of fewer than six.
Via Pirandello 37. www.trattoriadanino.com. ✆ **0942-21265.** Main courses 8€–18€. Daily noon–3pm and 6:30–11pm.

Vecchia Taormina ★★ SICILIAN   One of Taormina's longtime favorites keeps a steady stream of regulars happy with what are reputed to be the best pizzas around. The *pizza alla Norma,* the ingredients of the classic Sicilian pasta on a flaky crust, makes good on the claim. The kitchen also does nice versions of spaghetti con vongole (with clams), or topped with fresh sardines and breadcrumbs, as well as other classics, and serves them in two cozy rooms and a delightful multilevel terrace in an alleyway outside.
Vico Ebre 3. ✆ **0942-625589.** Main courses 10€–15€. Thurs–Tues 7:30–10:30pm.

Outdoor Pursuits

To reach the best and most popular beach, **Lido Mazzarò,** you have to go south of town via a cable car (✆ **0942-23605**) that leaves from Via Pirandello every 15 minutes (3€ round-trip). This soft, finely pebbled beach is one of the best equipped in Sicily, with bars, restaurants, and hotels. You can rent beach chairs, umbrellas, and watersports equipment at kiosks from April to October. To the right of Lido Mazzarò, past the Capo Sant'Andrea headland, is the region's prettiest cove, where twin crescents of beach sweep from a sand spit out to the minuscule **Isola Bella** islet.

North of Mazzarò are the long, wide beaches of **Spisone** and **Letojanni,** more developed but less crowded than **Giardini,** the large, built-up resort beach south of Isola Bella. A local bus leaves Taormina for

Mazzarò, Spisone, and Letojanni, and another heads down the coast to Giardini.

Shopping

Shopping is all too easy in Taormina—just walk along **Corso Umberto I**. Ceramics are one of Sicily's most notable handicrafts, and Taormina's shops are among the best places to buy them on the island, as the selection is excellent. **Giuseppa di Blasi,** Corso Umberto I 103 (✆ **0942-24671**), has a nice range of designs and specializes in the highly valued "white pottery" from Caltagirone. Mixing the new and the old, **Carlo Panarello Antichità,** Corso Umberto I 122 (✆ **0942-23910**), offers Sicilian ceramics (from pots to tables) and also deals in eclectic antique furnishings, paintings, and engravings.

Side Trips from Taormina

CASTELMOLA

Taormina gets high praise for its gorgeous views, but for connoisseurs of scenic outlooks, the real show takes place in the village of Castelmola, an eagle's nest 3km (2 miles) northwest of Taormina, and about 300m (1,000 ft.) feet higher. The Ionian Sea seems to stretch to the ends of the earth from up here, and you'll be staring right into the northern flanks of Mount Etna. For the full experience, make the trip up on foot, following routes that begin at Porta Catania and Porta Messina (the tourist office or any hotel desk can give you directions); the Porta Messina trail passes a section of the Roman aqueduct and the Convento dei Cappuccini, where you can pause for views and a breather. Either route involves an hour or so of fairly strenuous walking, but once at the top, stop at Castelmola's **Bar Turrisi** (Piazza Duomo 19; ✆ **0942-28181**; 10am–1am,

You can hike, drive or take a bus up to Castelmola.

and until 3am weekends and holidays) for a glass of *vino alla mandorla* (almond wine) and a look at its peculiar art collection. If that's more walking than you care to do, you can also drive up to Castelmola (park below the village and walk in) or take an orange local bus that runs more or less hourly from Porta Messina (2.20€ round-trip).

GOLE DELL'ALCANTARA

In a series of narrow gorges on the Alcantara (Al-*cahn*-ta-rah) river, rushing ice-cold water fed by snow melt on Mount Etna darts and dashes over fantastically twisted volcanic rock, creating a scenic spectacle that's especially refreshing on a hot day. The basalt rock formations were sculpted into these wild shapes thousands of years ago by cool water flowing over molten debris during eruptions on Mount Etna. The gorge is now protected as **Parco Fluviale dell'Alcanta** (www. parcoalcantara.it; ✆ **0942-985010**), though ticket booths, turnstiles, and elevators into the gorge lend an amusement-park aura. You can get away from the crowds with a hike along the riverbed, stopping now and then to lounge on flat riverside rocks and wade and even swim in the chill water. From October to April, only the upper area of the park, with an overlook trail above the gorge, is open. It costs 8€ to enter the park (open daily 7am–7:30pm). Amenities include a gift shop, cafeteria, picnic areas, and toilets. You can reach the Gole dell'Alcantara by car from Taormina (a 35-min. drive) or you can take **Interbus** (www. interbus.it; © **0942-625301**) for the 1-hour trip, with several daily departures from Taormina. The round-trip fare is 6€. Organized excursions (from 25€) to the gorges are also offered by many bus tour operators in Taormina, often in conjunction with a visit to Mount Etna.

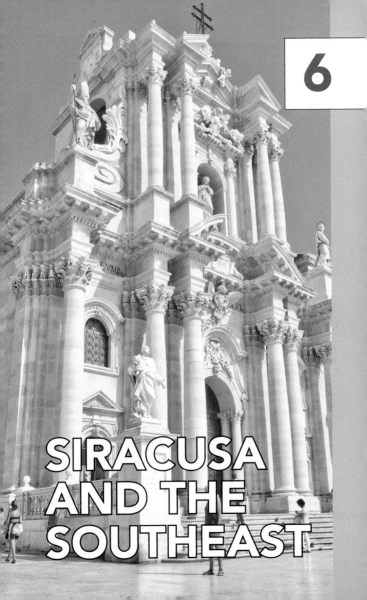

SIRACUSA AND THE SOUTHEAST

Siracusa (Syracuse) retains copious ruins and enough of its grandeur to suggest its role as one of the chief cities of the ancient world of Magna Graecia (Greater Greece). This rather exotic seaside city, especially its old core on Ortygia island, is also filled with baroque palaces and churches. For a real taste of the baroque, though, you need to head inland, to Noto and Ragusa.

SIRACUSA ★★

This small, out-of-the-way southern city packs a one-two punch. Siracusa was one of the most important cities of Magna Graecia (Greater Greece), rivaling even Athens in power and influence, and the still-functioning Teatro Greco, where Aeschylus premiered his plays, is one of many landmarks of the ancient metropolis. The charming historical center, on miniscule Ortigia Island, belongs to a much later time, the 18th century, when palaces and churches were built in an ebullient baroque style following the earthquake of 1693.

Siracusa might seem far removed, but in making the trip to the southeast coast you'll be following in the illustrious footsteps of the scientist Archimedes, statesman Cicero, evangelist St. Paul, martyr St. Lucy, painter Caravaggio, and naval hero Admiral Lord Horatio Nelson, all of whom left a mark on this rather remarkable place.

PREVIOUS PAGE: **Siracusa.**

Essentials

GETTING THERE   Siracusa is 1½ hours south of Taormina on the A18. It's 3 hours southeast of Palermo on the A19 and A18, and 3 hours east of Agrigento on the SS540, A19, and A18. Siracusa is also well connected with the rest of Sicily by bus and train, though buses are generally more efficient and frequent than trains. **Interbus buses** (www.etnatrasporti.it) run almost hourly between Siracusa and Catania and several times a day between Siracusa and Palermo. Train travel usually requires a change in Cantania; for information, contact www.trenitalia.com ✆ **892021.** Both trains and buses arrive in Siracusa at the station on Via Francesco Crispi, centrally located between the Parco Archeologico (Archaeological Park) and Ortygia.

GETTING AROUND   You won't need a car, just your own two feet and perhaps a few bus or cab rides to see the best of Siracusa proper. However, if you're using Siracusa as a base for exploring southeastern Sicily, you may arrive here by car—in which case, inquire about parking with your hotel or rental agency before arriving.

VISITOR INFORMATION   The **tourist office,** at Via San Sebastiano 43 (✆ **0931-481232**), is open Monday to Friday 8:30am to 1:30pm and 3 to 6pm, Saturday 8:30am to 1:30pm. There's another office in the historic center at Via della Maestranza 33 (✆ **0931-65201**); it's open Monday to Friday 8:15am to 2pm and 2:30 to 5:30pm, Saturday 8:15am to 2pm.

Exploring Siracusa

Ortigia Island is Siracusa's *centro storico,* a mostly pedestrian zone where narrow alleys lined with romantic 18th-century *palazzi* spill onto Piazza del Duomo, the most beautiful square in Sicily. The ancient ruins lie a good half-hour walk north of Ortigia along Corso Gelone.

ORTIGIA ISLAND ★★★

The historic center of Siracusa is an island only about 1 sq. km (¾ sq. mile), with breezy, palm-shaded seaside promenades fringing its shores. Most of the island is baroque, with grandiose palaces and churches lining narrow lanes and flamboyant piazzas, though Ortigia was settled in ancient times—as ancients believed, when Leto stopped by to give birth to Artemis, one of the twins she conceived with Zeus (she continued on her way and delivered Apollo on the Greek island of Delos).

The first landmark you'll come to after you cross Ponte Umbertino from the mainland is the **Temple of Apollo,** the oldest Doric temple in Sicily. The Apollion would have measured 58m × 24m (190 ft. × 79 ft.) when it was built in the 6th century B.C. It later served as a Byzantine church, then a mosque, then a church again under the Normans and is now an evocative

Siracusa's Ortigia Island.

Siracusa's Piazza del Duomo is considered one of the most handsome plazas in all of Italy.

ruin, with the temple platform, a fragmentary colonnade, and an inner wall rising in the middle of Piazza Pancali.

The **Piazza del Duomo,** one of the most beautiful squares in Sicily, is all about theatrics—a sea of white marble softened by pink oleander and surrounded by flamboyant palaces enlivened with elaborate stone filigree work and wrought-iron balconies. The Duomo itself (open daily 8am–noon and 4–7pm) is frothily baroque, almost too playful to be religious. The two tiers of tall Doric columns that define its remarkable facade were originally part of Siracusa's 5th-century B.C. Temple of Athena, one of the best-known sights of the ancient world, built to celebrate a Greek victory over the Carthaginians. Cicero, the Roman orator and traveler, reported that the temple was filled with gold, the doors were made of gold and ivory, and a statue of Athena atop the pediment was visible for miles out to sea. Romans made off with the gold, but a statue of the Virgin stands atop the pediment like Athena once did. Other ancient columns are a looming presence in

SIRACUSA AND THE SOUTHEAST

the apse of the church, which was first fashioned from the temple around the 7th century.

On the south side of the square is the pretty church of **Santa Lucia alla Badia,** with a tall, marble baroque facade embellished with twisted columns, pediments, and a wrought-iron balcony. Lucia, a plucky 4th-century Siracusan virgin, is the city's patron; born of wealth, from an early age she adapted Christian principles and was determined to give her worldly goods to the poor. Her piousness and generosity annoyed the young man to whom she had once been betrothed, and out of spite for seeing Lucia's sizable dowry squandered in such a way, the youth denounced her to Roman authorities. Lucia was condemned to prostitution, but refused to be dragged off to a brothel. Authorities then tied her to a pillar and lit a fire beneath her, but she proved to be flame resistant. Finally, a soldier plunged a sword into her throat. You'll see depictions of this gruesome act throughout Siracusa and the rest of Sicily, where the saint is very popular (tamer versions show the saint holding the sword that killed her).

Also on Piazza del Duomo is an entrance to the **Hypogeum** (no phone; admission 3€; Tues–Sun 9am–1pm and 4–8pm), a network of underground chambers and corridors dug as air-raid shelters in World War II.

Historians spout some mumbo-jumbo about the water that feeds **Fonte Aretusa,** a lovely shoreline spot where papyrus grows in a shallow pool fed by a spring that supplied Siracusa with fresh water for millennia. Classical myth, however, tells a different story: The nymph Aretusa was bathing in a river in Greece when the river god Alpheus took a liking to her. She asked for help in avoiding his advances, and Artemis,

The Burial of St. Lucy in the Galleria Regionale Palazzo Bellomo.

goddess of the wilderness and protectress of young women, turned her into a river that emerged here. Not to be thwarted, Alpheus followed suit, and the two of them bubble forth for eternity.

The elegant 13th-century palace **Galleria Regionale Palazzo Bellomo** (Via Capodieci 16; ℂ **0931-69511**; admission 8€; Tues–Sat 9am–7pm, Sun 9am–1pm), houses Sicilian works from the Middle Ages through the 20th century, including two great masterpieces. Antonello da Messina's **"Annunciation"** (1474) shows the artist's remarkable attention to detail: Tall windows, beams, columns, the Virgin's bed, and a blue-and-white vase compose an intricately rendered interior, with bright light infusing the spaces. The scene is typical of the Flemish paintings that were popular in Naples, where Messina studied when he left his native Sicily while still a teenager. Caravaggio's **"Burial of St. Lucia"** was commissioned in the late fall of 1608, when the artist had just escaped from a prison in Malta and come to Siracusa. Note how, with his characteristic lighting, the artist highlights the muscular gravediggers, showing their brute strength, while the mourners seem small and meek in the background. A shaft of light falls on Lucia's face and neck, showing the stab wound that killed her; she is a study in serenity, having entered the heavenly kingdom.

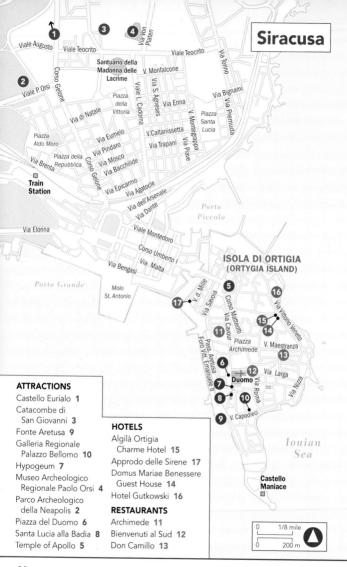

Siracusa

THE ANCIENT RUINS ★★★

Of all the Greek cities of antiquity that flourished in Sicily, Siracusa was the most important, a formidable competitor of Athens. In its heyday, it dared take on Carthage and even Rome. Sprawling Greek and Roman ruins are these days surrounded by an unremarkable section of the modern city. To reach the ruins, walk north along Corso Gelone (or better yet, take bus no. 1, 3, or 12, or a cab from Ortigia's Piazza Pancali) or take buses 11, 25, or 26 from the front of Siracusa's central train station.

Castello Eurialo ★ RUINS Part of a massive, 27km (16-mi) long defense system, this 4th-century B.C. fortress is surrounded by three trenches, connected by underground tunnels. These supposedly impregnable defenses were never put to the test: Siracusa fell to the Romans in 212 B.C. without a fight, because the entire garrison was celebrating the feast of Aphrodite. Legend has it that it was here that the Greek mathematician Archimedes famously cried "Eureka!" having discovered the law of water displacement while taking a bath. The evocative ruin overlooking the Siracusan plain is the best-preserved Greek castle in the Mediterranean. The defenses are at the far end of the archaeological zone, about 5km (3 miles) outside the city center near a village called Belvedere; buses 25 and 26 along Corso Gelone pass the entrance.

Piazza Eurialo 1, off Viale Epipoli in the Belvedere district. ℂ **0931-481111.** Admission 4€; 10€ when combined with Parco Archeologico and Museo Archeologico. Daily 9am–5:30pm.

Catacombe di San Giovanni ★★ RUINS Spooky subterranean chambers, installed in underground aqueducts that had been abandoned by the Greeks, contain some 20,000 ancient Christian tombs. They are entered through the Church of San Giovanni, now in ruin but holy ground for centuries; it was the city's cathedral until it was more or less leveled by an earthquake in 1693. St. Paul allegedly preached here when he stopped in Siracusa around A.D. 59, and a church was erected to commemorate the event in the 6th century. The Cripta di San Marciano (Crypt of St. Marcian) honors a popular Siracusan martyr, a 1st-century A.D. bishop who was tied to a pillar and flogged to death on this spot.

Piazza San Giovanni, at end of Viale San Giovanni. No phone. Admission 5€. Tues–Sun 9:30am–12:30pm and 2:30–4:30pm. Closed Feb.

Museo Archeologico Regionale Paolo Orsi (Paolo Orsi Regional Archaeological Museum) ★★★ MUSEUM

One of Italy's finest archaeological collections shows off artifacts from southern Sicily's prehistoric inhabitants through the

Artifacts on display at the Museo Archeologico Regionale Paolo Orsi.

Romans, showcasing pieces in stunning modern surroundings. Amid prehistoric tools and sculptures are the skeletons of a pair of dwarf elephants, as intriguing to us as they were to the ancients: It's believed that the large central orifice (nasal passage) of these skeletal beasts inspired the myth of the one-eyed Cyclops. Early Greeks left behind a (much-reproduced) grinning terracotta Gorgon that once adorned the frieze of the temple of Athena (see **Duomo**, p. 95) to ward off evil. You'll also see scores of votive cult statuettes devoted to Demeter and Persephone—mother and daughter goddesses linked to fertility and the harvest. Legend had it that Hades, god of the underworld, abducted Persephone in Sicily and carried her down to his realm; with a bit of negotiating between angry Demeter and the other gods, it was agreed that Persephone could return to Earth but must descend to resume her duties as queen of the underworld for part of the year, when in her absence winter descends upon the lands above. The museum's most celebrated piece is the **Landolina Venus**, a Roman copy of an original by the great classical Greek sculptor Praxiteles. The graceful and modest goddess, now headless, rises out of marble waves; French writer Guy de Maupassant, visiting in 1885, called her "the perfect expression of exuberant beauty."

In the gardens of the Villa Landolina in Akradina, Viale Teocrito 66. ✆ **0931-464022.** Admission 8€ or 14€ with combo ticket that includes Parco Archeologico della Neapolis. Tues–Sat 9am–6pm; Sun 9am–1pm.

Parco Archeologico della Neapolis ★★★ RUINS

Many of Siracusa's ancient ruins are clustered in this archaeological park at the western edge of town, immediately north of Stazione Centrale.

A Gigantic Teardrop Runs Through It

The tallest building in Siracusa is the bizarre **Santuario della Madonna delle Lacrime** (Our Lady of Tears Sanctuary, Via Santuario 33; ℂ **0931-21446;** free admission; daily 8am–noon and 4–7pm), a monstrous cone of contemporary architecture (built in 1993) halfway between Ortigia and the archaeological zone. Meant to evoke a sort of angular teardrop and rising 74m (243 ft.) with a diameter of 80m (262 ft.), it houses a statue of the Madonna that supposedly wept for 5 days in 1953. Alleged chemical tests showed that the liquid was similar to that of human tears. Pilgrims flock here, and you'll see postcards of the weepy Virgin around Siracusa. In the interior, vertical windows stretch skyward to the apex of the roof. A charlatan TV evangelist and his rapt congregation would not look out of place here.

The **Teatro Greco** ★★★ (Greek Theater) was hewn out of bedrock in the 5th century B.C., with 67 rows that could seat 16,000 spectators. It was reconstructed in the 3rd century B.C., appears now much as it did then, and is still the setting for ancient drama in the spring and early summer. Tickets cost 30€ to 70€. For information, contact **INDA,** Corso Matteotti 29, Siracusa (www.indafondazione.org; ℂ **0931-487200**).

Only the ancient theaters in Rome and Verona are larger than the **Anfiteatro Romano,** created during the rein of Augustus, around 20 B.C. Gladiators sparred here, and a square hole in the center of the arena suggests that machinery was used to lift wild beasts from below. Some historical evidence suggests that the arena could be flooded for mock sea battles called *naumachiae;* pumps could also have flooded and drained a reservoir in which crocodiles are said to have

Neapolis Archeological Park.

fed on the corpses of victims killed in the games. The Spanish carted off much of the stonework to rebuild the city fortifications when they conquered Siracusa in the 16th century, but some of the seats remain—the first rows would have been reserved for Roman citizens, those right above for wealthy Siracusans, and the last rows for the hoi polloi.

What is now a lush grove of lemon and orange trees, the **Latomia del Paradiso** (Quarry of Paradise) was at one time a fearsome place, vast, dark, and subterranean—until the cavern's roof collapsed in the great earthquake of 1693. Originally prisoners were worked to death here to quarry the stones used in the construction of ancient Siracusa. Certainly the most storied attraction in the park is the **Orecchio di Dionisio** (Ear of Dionysius). The Greeks created this tall and vaguely ear-shaped cave by digging into the cliff, simply to expand the limestone quarry for water storage—but something about this huge cavern has always inspired more dramatic accounts. When the flamboyant painter Caravaggio lived in Siracusa in the early 17th century, he playfully dubbed the cavern the Ear of Dionysus, after the 5th- to 4th-century B.C. ruler of Greek Siracusa, and backed that up with a wild story:

that Dionysus had imprisoned political opponents in the cave because of its unique acoustic effect—he could sit near the opening and hear every word they said. Other legends, completely unfounded, say the cave's occupants were Athenians captured by Dionysus' mercenaries during the Peloponnesian Wars; this version claims that he liked the way the cave's acoustics amplified their screams as they were tortured. Almost as fascinating is the well-documented purpose of the **Ara di Ierone** (or, Altar of Heron): Fifth-century B.C. Greeks built the altar, 196m (636 ft.) long and 23m (75 ft.) wide and approached by enormous ramps, for the sacrifice of 450 bulls at one time.

Via Del Teatro (off the intersection of Corso Gelone and Viale Teocrito), Viale Paradiso. ✆ **0931-66206.** Admission 10€ or 14€ with combo ticket that includes archaeological museum. Daily 9am–6pm (until 4:30pm on certain summer evenings when performances are held in the theater).

Where to Stay

The best place to stay in Siracusa is Ortigia, with enough character, charm, and comfortable choices to keep the most discerning traveler happy. A good agency for apartments in Ortigia is **Case Sicilia** (www.casesicilia.com; ✆ **339-2983507**). For villas, **Think Sicily** (www.thinksicily.com) has a carefully edited list of well-equipped properties in and around Siracusa.

Algilà Ortigia Charme Hotel ★   A slightly exotic air pervades this old stone palace at the edge of the sea. Built around a peaceful inner courtyard with a splashing fountain, it's accented throughout with carefully restored stone work and wooden beams, offset by beautiful multicolor tiles and other rich details. Rooms combine conventional luxury, with all the modern amenities, and a surfeit of four-poster beds, antiques, and tribal kilims; many have sea views. The in-house restaurant serves Sicilian classics and seafood beneath a beautiful wooden ceiling.

Via Vittorio Veneto 93. www.algila.it. © **0931-465186.** 30 units. 174€–400€ double. Rates include buffet breakfast. **Amenities:** Restaurant; room service; Wi-Fi (free, in lobby).

Approdo delle Sirene ★★

This natty little inn occupies two floors of a seaside apartment house, beautifully refashioned as light-filled quarters with a slightly nautical flair, as becomes the sparking blue water just beyond the tall windows. In the contemporary-styled guest rooms, polished wood floors offset handsome blond furnishings, striped fabrics, and bold colors. Several rooms have French doors opening to small balconies, though some rooms are sky-lit only—flooded with light but without outlooks. The sunny breakfast room/lounge and terrace provide plenty of views, however. The hosts, a mother-and-son team, Fiora and Friedrich, are a hospitable on-the-scene presence and can arrange all kinds of tours and excursions. They even have bikes available for guests' use (no charge).

Riva Garibaldi 15. www.apprododellesirene.com. © **0931-24857.** 8 units. 80€–130€ double. 2-night minimum stay June–Aug. Rates include buffet breakfast. **Amenities:** Bikes, Wi-Fi (free).

Domus Mariae Benessere Guest House ★

The Ursiline sisters who still occupy a wing of this seaside convent have found their calling as innkeepers. They provide large, bright rooms that are functional bordering on vaguely luxurious, with plush headboards on extremely comfortable beds, attractive rugs on tile floors, and lots of counter and storage space in the large bathrooms. Some rooms have sea views, while others face an atrium-like courtyard. Some surprising indulgences given the surroundings are a lovely roof terrace and a lower level spa, with a small pool and Jacuzzi available to all guests. An in-house restaurant serves a rather monastic breakfast (included in room rates, though coffee is extra) as well as a well-prepared dinner featuring healthful Mediterranean fare.

Via Veneto 89. www.domusmariaebenessere.com. ✆ **0931-24854.** 21 units. From 60€ double. Rates include buffet breakfast. **Amenities:** Bikes (free), pool, Wi-Fi (free).

Hotel Gutkowski ★★

Two old houses facing the sea at the edge of Ortigia are warm, hospitable, and capture the essence of southern Italy—Sicilian hues on the walls, colorful floor tiles, and views of the blue water or sun baked roofs of the old city. Each room is different, some with balconies, some with terraces, and furnishings throughout are functional but chosen with care to provide restful simplicity—old Sicilian and vintage mid-century pieces offset contemporary tables and bedsteads. A rooftop terrace serves as an outdoor living room for much of the year, and the bar serves not only regional wines but also one or two well-prepared dishes in the evenings for guests only.

Lungomare Vittorini 26. www.guthotel.it. ✆ **0931-465861.** 25 units. From 90€ double. Rates include buffet breakfast. **Amenities:** Bar; Wi-Fi (free).

Where to Eat

Caseificio Borderi, tucked in among piles of fresh fish in Ortigia's colorful morning market at 6 Via die Benedictis (✆ **329-9852500**), is a mandatory stop on the food circuit for its huge selection of house-made cheeses, cured meats, olives, and wine; the staff hands out samples and makes delicious sandwiches (about 3€).

Archimede ★★ SEAFOOD   This Siracusa institution has been serving meals in white-washed, vaulted dining rooms since 1938; it's remained a favorite for a night out, even through those long post-war years when the surrounding neighborhood moldered in neglect. Specialties veer toward such Sicilian classics as spaghetti with *ricci* (sea urchin), tagliolini al *nero di seppie* (pasta with cuttlefish ink), and *pesce all'acqua pazza* (fish cooked with garlic, tomatoes, capers, and olives); many fans claim that no one in Sicily makes them better. The kitchen is also equipped with a wood-fired oven that turns out what many Siracusans consider to be the best pizza in town, available in different sizes, including one that's perfect as a starter.
Via Gemmallaro 8. www.trattoriaarchimede.it. ⓒ **0931-69701.** Main courses 12€–24€. Mon–Sat 12:30–3:30pm and 7:30–11:30pm.

Bienvenuti al Sud ★ SICILIAN/CREATIVE   Sicilian towns are full of casual eateries like this—barebones storefronts with open kitchens and plastic tables. Locals know the ones that serve the best food, and this simple, four-table room operated by an enthusiastic young husband-and-wife team is one of Ortigia's hidden gems (it's on a back street behind the Duomo). Chef Christian serves the specialties you'd encounter in a Sicilian home and he enhances the homey ambience as he chats from the kitchen while he prepares linguine al neonate (baby fish), fresh from the market fish baked with capers and olives, and a simple but delicious gnocchi alla Palermitana, with eggplant, mozzarella, and tomatoes. Dinner is often followed by a complimentary glass of almond wine.

Via della Concillazione 22. ✆ **0931-64046.** Main courses 9€–12€. Daily 7pm–midnight, lunch some days.

Don Camillo ★★ SIRACUSAN/SEAFOOD The top contender with Archimede (see above) for old-time Siracusa favorite is slightly more formal, with lots of polished antiques offsetting the handsomely tiled floors and rows of vintage wines. House specialties, like spaghetti *delle Sirene* (with sea urchin and shrimp in butter) and *tagliata al tonno* (with sliced tuna), have been drawing loyal regulars here for years. On weekends especially, join the many Siracusan families who fill the vaulted rooms decorated with vintage photos of Ortigia.

Via Maestranza 96. www.ristorantedoncamillosiracusa.it. ✆ **0931-67133.** Main courses 14€–24€. Mon–Sat 12:30–3pm and 7:30–10:30pm.

Side Trips from Siracusa
BEACHES NEAR SIRACUSA

Some of the best, unspoiled shoreline in all of Italy is on Sicily's southeastern coast. **Fontane Bianche** is the closest beach to Siracusa, 15 minutes away. It's an almost-square bay with laid-back beach clubs and luxurious deep sand. **Lido di Noto,** 15 minutes from the baroque hill town of Noto, is a lively beach with great waterfront restaurants. Half the beach is private beach clubs (where you pay around 10€ for day use of a lounge chair, umbrella, and shower facilities), and half is free public access. Between Noto and Pachino is the **Vendicari Nature Reserve,** where beaches are small and hard to find but the scenery is beautiful. Thousands of migratory birds nest here every year. A few miles south of the autostrada on SP19, park at the

Agriturismo Calamosche to reach **Calamosche**. It's a 15-minute walk down a nature path to reach the intimate cove, framed by rock cliffs and sea caves. The water is a calm, perfectly dappled teal. **Isola delle Correnti ★★**, a little over an hour south of Siracusa at the southeastern tip of the island, is one of the best beaches on Sicily. It's a bit more windswept and wavy than the other spots. On a clear day, you can see Malta, which is just 100km (60 miles) to the south.

NOTO ★★★
31km (19 miles) SW of Siracusa

Dubbed the "Stone Garden" because of its sheer beauty, this little town has a main street, Corso Vittorio Emanuele, lined with rich-looking buildings of golden stone, some of the most captivating on the island. What's more, Noto is set amid olive groves and

The hill town of Noto.

almond trees on a plateau overlooking the Asinaro Valley, providing lovely outlooks.

GETTING THERE Take the A18 autostrada south for 27km (17 miles), then exit and head north up a hill, following blue signs toward Noto. Near town, be sure to follow the yellow signs toward Noto's *"centro storico"* (brown "Noto Antica" signs lead to the ruins of the old city, quite some distance from town.) The drive from Siracusa takes about 35 minutes. It's also easy to reach Noto by bus (55 min. each way; 6€ round-trip), with either **AST** (www.aziendasicilianatrasporti.it) or **Interbus** (www.interbus.it), which offer about a dozen buses per day from Ortigia or Siracusa train station. Buses arrive at Noto's Piazzale Marconi, a 5-minute walk from the *centro storico*.

VISITOR INFORMATION The **tourist office** at Via Gioberti 13 (© **0931-836503**) is open May to September daily from 9am to 1pm and 3:30 to 6:30pm; from October to April it's open Monday through Friday, 8am to 2pm and 3:30 to 6:30pm.

Exploring Noto

Noto, a hill town on the flanks of Mount Alviria, was a flourishing place in the late 17th century, having outgrown its medieval core and expanded into new streets lined with palaces and convents. Then, on January 11, 1693, it all came tumbling down, as the strongest earthquake in Italian history leveled Noto and much of the rest of southeastern Sicily. The ruins of that old city can be seen at the "Noto Antica" archaeological site outside of town.

The good to come out of such a devastating tragedy, however, is that Noto was rebuilt—not on the same site but on the banks of the River Asinaro, and not haphazardly, but in splendid, unified baroque style. Noto is a stage-set of honey-colored limestone, with curvaceous facades, curling staircases, and potbellied wrought-iron balconies. You will be surrounded by all this theatricality on a walk down **Corso Vittorio Emanuele III**, though things hit a high note on a side street, **Via Nicolaci.** Be sure not to miss the beautiful elliptical facade of the **Chiesa di Montevirgine** church, and the playful **Palazzo Villadorata** (or Palazzo Nicolaci), where expressive maidens, dwarves, lions, and horses support the balconies.

Work on the 18th-century landmarks is ongoing (the **Duomo** was just rebuilt after a 1997 collapse), while much of the rest of the town seems to languish in disrepair—suggesting that in Noto the attitude is, "If it ain't baroque, don't fix it."

RAGUSA ★

79km (49 miles) SW of Siracusa.

Ragusa is a town divided, between modern Ragusa Superiore and baroque Ragusa Ibla. The two are separated by a deep ravine, the Valle dei Ponti. The divide came about in 1693, when a powerful earthquake all but obliterated Ragusa Ibla, the original town, killing thousands. Despite efforts to rebuild Ragusa Ibla as a planned town in exuberant baroque style, most of the wary residents decided to relocate to an adjacent ridge, calling their new settlement Ragusa Superiore. Today, Ragusa Superiore is the modern center of the sprawling, two-parted town. Two-sided Ragusa is an inviting place to wander—from Ragusa Superiore into Ragusa Ibla, and once there along quiet lanes and shady piazzas enlivened with the flamboyant baroque facades of churches. From the twin towns, you'll often catch glimpses of the surrounding countryside, where

Ragusa's splendid cathedral.

fields and orchards are crisscrossed with low-lying, white, dry-stone walls.

Essentials

GETTING THERE From Siracusa, three **trains** per day make the 2-hour journey to Ragusa. **AST buses** (www.aziendasiciliatrasporti.it; ℘ **0932-681818**) make the three-hour run seven times per day. The train and bus stations are in Ragusa Superiore on Piazza del Popolo and the adjoining Piazza Gramsci.

By **car** from Siracusa, the quickest route takes you through Noto (p. 109) then southwest along Route 115 to the town of Ispica, at which point the highway swings northwest toward Ragusa.

VISITOR INFORMATION The **tourist office,** Via Capitano Bocchieri 33 (© **0932-221511**), is open Monday, Wednesday, and Friday 9am to 1:30pm and Tuesday and Thursday 9am to 1:30pm and 4 to 6pm.

GETTING AROUND If you don't want to make the steep climb linking Ibla with Superiore, you can take city bus no. 3 departing from in front of the cathedral or from Piazza del Popolo in Superiore. It's a hair-raising ride. The bus will let you off in Ibla at Piazza Pola or Giardini Iblei, which are most central for exploring the medieval and baroque town.

What to See & Do

The most scenic way to reach the old town is by taking the 242 steps of the Salita Commendatore that clamor down the hillside from Ragusa Superiore into Ragusa Ibla. You can take a breather along the way on a landing in front of the ruined **Santa Maria delle Scale** (St. Mary of the Steps), enjoying the views of the ochre-colored houses of Ragusa Ibla spreading out at your feet.

The path eventually winds around to **Piazza del Duomo,** where a dramatically curved staircase leads to the sumptuous façade of **Cattedrale di San Giorgio ★★** (© **0932-220-085**), open daily 9am to noon and 4 to 7pm. Three tiers of columns and balconies are the piece de resistance of architect Rosario Gagliardi, the master of the Sicilian baroque. Gagliardi's second-best work is just east, **Chiesa di San Giuseppe ★,** Via Torre Nuova 19 (© **0932-621779**), open daily from 9am to noon and 4 to 6pm. The tall, convex façade rises in three-tiers, embellished with

The Ibleo Gardens.

columns and statues of saints. Inside, above a striking floor of black asphalt interspersed with majolica tiles, is one Ragusa's most beloved paintings, so-called "Our Lady of the Cherries." In an altarpiece portraying the Holy Family, Mary appears to be holding cherries in her apron and offering them to passersby.

Just down the street are the beautiful public gardens, **Giardino Ibleo ★★.** Long avenues lined with date palms are idyllic places to stroll, and stone benches are tucked into shady alcoves. At the edge of the gardens, a terrace opens to sweeping views across the Valley of Irminio. The gardens can be visited daily from 8am to 8pm; admission is free.

Where to Stay & Eat

La Bettola ★★ SICILIAN   The 1940s-era décor suggests simpler times, and the Sicilian classics that arrives at tables bedecked with red-checked table-cloths in the homey dining room and on the large terrace in front don't do anything to shake off the throwback ambiance. Daily offerings are listed on a chalkboard—homemade salamis and caponata, octopus salad, big platters of spaghetti a la Norma, simply grilled pork cutlets topped with fresh herbs.

Largo Camerina 7. ℰ **0932-653377.** Main courses 10€–15€. Mon–Sat 12:30–2:30pm and 7:30–11:30pm.

Locanda Don Serafino ★ SICILIAN   The vaulted, rock-walled cellars are the evocative setting for a grand meal, and the mazelike guest rooms are wonderfully

A unique, cavelike guestroom at Locanda Don Serafino.

cool in the dog days of summer. The food is more traditional and down to earth than the fancy décor and
lavish table settings might suggest. A rich *zuppa di
pesce don Serafino* (fish soup) and such meat-heavy
dishes as hare, roasted with mountain herbs, can be
coupled with fresh fish steamed in zucchini leaves. In
July and August the restaurant does not serve lunch.

Via Orfanotrofio 39. www.locandadonserafino.it. ℂ **0932-
220065.** Main courses 30€–35€. Wed–Mon 12:30–2:30pm and
5:30–11:30pm.

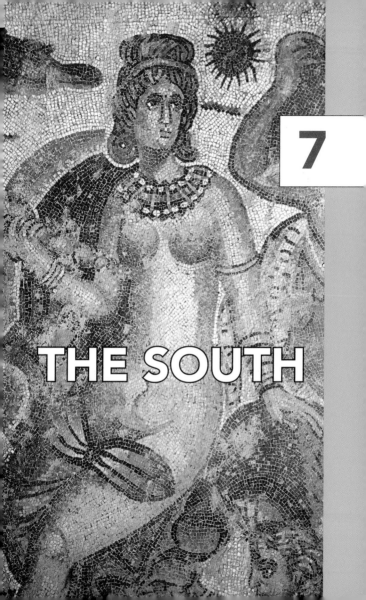

7

THE SOUTH

It's easy to think of the rugged coast, plains, and hinterlands of southern Sicily as undiscovered, but that's only relative. Granted, these lands have little of the sophistication of Taormina or the urban clamor of Palermo, but to consider them unexplored backwaters is to forget history. The Greeks and after them the Romans found their way here millennia ago. The Greeks built magnificent cities in Agrigento and Selinunte, and their well-preserved temples still stand. Meanwhile, the Romans left a rich collection of mosaics at the Villa del Casale, outside Piazza Armerina. If you're making a sweep through the south, it's easiest to reach these far-flung attractions by car. By public transport, they're most easily accessible from Palermo.

PIAZZA ARMERINA ★★★

134km (83) miles NW of Siracusa, 158km (98 miles) SE of Palermo

Why do travelers make such an effort to get to this dusty, sun-baked hilltown in the center of Sicily? There's one very simple reason: To see the richest collection of Roman mosaics in the world, at the **Villa del Casale**, in the countryside 5km (3 miles) outside of town. Here, from elevated walkways you'll gaze

PREVIOUS PAGE: **A mosaic in Piazza Amerina's Villa Romana del Casale.**

down upon wild beasts, bikini-clad exercisers, super-heroes, and the monsters of myth, depicted in glorious and colorful mosaic tableaux. The masterful ancient craftsmanship is in a near-miraculous state of preservation, and provides a fascinating window into 4th-century A.D. preoccupations—but even more than that, looking at these brilliant mosaic scenes is as entertaining as watching a good film, one in glorious Technicolor.

Essentials

GETTING THERE   From Taormina, Siracusa, or anywhere in the east, take the A19 west from Catania, exit at Dittaino, and head south following blue signs for Piazza Armerina. From Palermo, take the A19 east and south, exit at Caltanissetta, then immediately look for signs for Piazza Armerina. (The route is SS626 south to SS122 east to SS117bis.) You can reach the nearby town of Piazza Armerina by **SAIS bus** (www.saisautolinee.it; *©* **800-211020**); from Palermo (a 2-hr trip) there are 5 buses a day, 3 on weekends; coming from Siracusa or other east coast towns, take a bus from Enna (40 min; 4 buses a day). Once in Piazza Armerina, take local bus B to the site (15 min; runs daily 9–noon and 3–6pm). Taxis also eagerly await visitors.

VISITOR INFORMATION   Admission to Villa Romana (Strada Provinciale 15; www.villaromanadelcasale.it; *©* **0935-680036**) is 10€. It's open daily 9am–7pm (until 5pm Nov–Mar).

Exploring Villa Romana del Casale

Built between 310 and 340, this enormous villa of a rich and powerful landowner was the center of a vast

Villa Romana del Casale.

agricultural estate. It was almost completely covered by a landslide in the 12th century, but this natural disaster turned out to be a blessing, as the mud preserved almost 38,000 square feet of mosaic flooring. Rediscovered in the 19th century, the glorious villa was excavated and restored beginning in the early 20th century.

The place must have been magnificent, more a palace than a mere villa, with 40 rooms, many of them clad in marble, frescoed, and equipped with fountains and pools. Terme, or steam baths (Rooms 1–7) heated the villa with steam circulating through cavities (now exposed) in the floors and walls. The villa was obviously built to impress, and the ostentation reached its height in the mosaics of mythology, hunting, flora and fauna, and domestic scenes that carpeted most of the floors. Given the style and craftsmanship, they were probably the work of master artists from North Africa.

The villa's 40 rooms are arranged around a garden courtyard, or peristyle. Take time as you wander through the rooms simply to enjoy the mosaics,

The "Room of the Fishing Cupids" at Villa Romana del Casale

noticing the expressions, colors, and playfulness of many of these scenes. Remember, the mosaics were intended to delight visitors.

Corridors of the **peristyle** (Room 13) contain the splendid Peristyle mosaic, a bestiary of birds, plants, wild animals, and more domesticated creatures such as horses. Adjoining it to the baths is the **Palestra** (exercise area, Room 15) where mosaics depict a chariot race at Rome's Circus Maximus.

Along the north side of the peristyle is the **Sala degli Eroti Pescatori ★** (Room of the Fishing Cupids, Room 24), probably a bedroom. The occupant would have drifted off to a busy scene of four boatloads of winged cupids harpooning, netting, and trapping various fish and sea creatures.

Just past those rooms is the **Sala della Piccola Caccia** (*Piccola caccia* meaning "small hunt," Room 25) where hunters in togas and leggings go after deer, wild boar, birds, and other small game as Diana, goddess of the hunt, looks on. In one scene the hunters roast their kill under a canopy.

The long hall to the east is the **Corridoio della Grande Caccia ★★★,** or Corridor of the Great Hunt (Room 28), measuring 65m (197 ft.) in length. The mosaics depict men capturing panthers, leopards, and other exotic animals, loading them onto wagons for transport, and finally onto a ship in an eastern-looking port. They're obviously bound for Rome, where they will be part of the games in the Colosseum.

A cluster of three rooms east of the north (right-hand side) end of the Grande Caccia corridor includes the **Vestibolo di Ulisse e Polifemo** (Vestibule of Ulysses and Polyphemus, Room 47), where the Homeric hero proffers a *krater* of wine to the Cyclops (here with three eyes instead of one, and a disemboweled ram draped casually over his lap) in hopes of getting him drunk. Adjacent is the **Cubicolo con Scena Erotica** (Bedroom with Erotic Scene, Room 46), where a seductress, with a side gaze and a nicely contoured rear end, embraces a young man.

Off the southwest side of the Grande Caccia corridor is one of the most amusing rooms of all, the **Sala delle Palestrite,** Room of the Gym Girls (Room 30). Their skimpy strapless bikinis would be appropriate for a beach in the 21st century, but ancient literary sources tell us that this was actually standard workout apparel 1,700 years ago—the bandeau top was called the *strophium,* and the bikini bottom the *subligar.* The girls are engaged in various exercises—curling dumbbells, tossing a ball, and running.

South of the central block of the villa and peristyle is the **Triclinium** (Room 33), a large dining room with a magnificent rendition of the Labors of Hercules. In the central apse, the mosaics depict the Gigantomachy (Battle of the Giants), in which five mammoth creatures are in their death throes after being pierced by Hercules's poisoned arrows.

AGRIGENTO & THE VALLEY OF THE TEMPLES ★★★

129km (80 miles) SE of Palermo

Colonists from Crete or Rhodes established Akragas in the 7th century B.C., and by the 5th century B.C. the city was one of the great Mediterranean powers, with close to 200,000 residents. The Greek poet Pindar described Akragas as the most beautiful city "inhabited by mortals" but commented that its citizens "feasted as if there were no tomorrow." The city poured part of its enormous wealth into temples erected along a ridge overlooking the sea, their bright pediments becoming well-known landmarks along southern sea routes. Carthage and Rome fought over the city for several centuries until Akragas became part of the Roman Empire in 210 B.C. Tumbled by earthquakes, plundered for marble, and overgrown from neglect, today the temples are merely proud remnants of ancient grandeur.

Columns from the ancient Temple of Hercules.

Visitors usually bypass the city itself, heading straight down to the temples. While modern, hilltop Agrigento is a fairly unappealing conglomeration of highways and concrete apartment blocks, a stroll around the small medieval center rewards you with a look at some atmospheric landmarks and a lively buzz.

Essentials

GETTING THERE Agrigento is about 2½ hours by **car** from either Palermo or Siracusa. From Palermo, cut southeast on the SS121, which becomes SS189 before it finally reaches Agrigento. From Siracusa, take the A18 autostrada north to Catania and the A19 west toward Enna; just past Enna, exit the A19 and follow signs south through Caltanissetta and down to Agrigento. The "coastal route" from Siracusa—taking the SS115 all the way—may look more direct on the map but is much more time-consuming, up to 5 hours on an often very curvy, two-lane road.

Bus connections between Palermo and Agrigento are fairly convenient: **Cuffaro** (www.cuffaro.info; ℂ **0922-403150**) runs nine buses per day each way and drops you right in front of the entrance to the archaeological site; the trip takes 2 hours and costs 8.30€ one-way or 13€ round-trip. Bus service from Siracusa takes at least 4 hours.

Taking the **train** to Agrigento is a hassle. The main rail station, **Stazione Centrale,** is at Piazza Marconi (ℂ **892021**); from there you then have to take a cab or local bus (lines 1, 2, or 3) to the temples, 10 minutes away. The train trip from Palermo takes 2 hours and costs 8€; there are 12 trains daily. From Siracusa, you must change in Catania; the full 6-hour trip costs 20€ one-way.

The Tempio della Concordia, Valley of the Temples, at Agrigento.

VISITOR INFORMATION The **tourist office,** in the modern town at Piazzale Aldo Moro 7 (*©* **0922-20454**), is open Sunday through Friday 8am to 1pm and 3 to 8pm, Saturday 8am to 1pm. Another tourist office is at Via Empedocle 73 (*©* **0922-20391**), open Monday to Friday 8am to 2:30pm and Wednesday also from 3:30 to 7pm.

Exploring the Ruins

The park is divided into eastern and western zones, with entrances at each.

Parco Valle dei Templei ★★★ RUINS In the eastern zone are Agrigento's three best-preserved temples. **The Temple of Hercules (Tempio di Ercole)** is the oldest, dating from the 6th century B.C. At one time the temple sheltered a celebrated statue of Hercules, though it has long since been plundered. Gaius Verres, the notoriously corrupt 1st-century B.C. governor of Sicily, had his eyes on the statue as he looted temples across the island, though there is no record of Verres (who was exiled for his misdeeds) getting this prize. Eight of 36 columns have been resurrected, while the others lie rather romantically scattered in the tall grass and wildflowers; they still bear black sears from fires set by Carthaginian invaders.

The **Tempio della Concordia (Temple of Concord),** surrounded by 34 columns, has survived almost intact since its completion in 430 B.C. It was never plundered because it was shored up as a Christian basilica in the 6th century, and its foundations rest on soft soil, absorbing the shock of earthquakes. The **Temple of Juno** had no such structural resiliency and was partly destroyed in an earthquake, though 30 columns and sections of the colonnade have been restored. A long altar was used for wedding ceremonies and sacrificial offerings.

The western zone would have been the setting of the largest temple in the Greek world, if the **Temple of Jove/Zeus (Tempio di Giove)** had ever been completed—and if what was built had not been toppled in earthquakes. A copy of an 8m-tall telamon (a sculpted figure of a man with arms raised) lies on its back amid the rubble; the original is the pride of the Museo Archeologico. The **Temple of Castor and Pollux (Tempio di Dioscuri** or **Tempio di Castore e Polluce),** with four Doric columns intact, honors Castor and Pollux, the twins who were patrons of seafarers; Demeter, the goddess of marriage and of the fertile earth; and Persephone, the daughter of Zeus and the symbol of spring. Parco Valle dei Templei. www.lavalledeitempli.eu. ℂ **0922-621611.** Admission 8€. Daily 8:30am–7pm. Separate admission 8€ for evening hours, July–Aug Mon–Fri until 9:30pm, Sat–Sun until 11pm; Sat until 11:30 rest of year.

Exploring the Modern City

Via Atenea is the main street of the modern city, worth a stroll for people watching and a look at small-town life, as lively here as it is anywhere else in Sicily.

Abbazia di Santo Spirito (Abbey of the Holy Spirit) ★ Giacomo Serpotta steals the show here. What Michelangelo was to marble sculpture, Serpotta was to stucco, and the artists made his contribution to the Sicilian baroque by creating white reliefs swirling with twisting figures (for more on Serpotta, see p. 32). Although the 13th-century church is rotting away, Serpotta's fantastic stucco-work scenes adorning a single nave are intact, depicting *The Adoration of the Magi*,

The Nativity, *The Presentation of Christ at the Temple*, and *The Flight into Egypt*. The cloisters are also a delight, and nuns in the adjoining convent sell a sweet confection called *kus-kus,* composed of chocolate and pistachio nuts.

Via Porcello at Via Santa Spirito. ✆ **0922-20664.** Free admission. Tues–Sat 9am–1pm and 4–7pm; Sun 9am–1pm.

Casa di Pirandello ★   The outlying birthplace of Luigi Pirandello, the 1934 Nobel Prize winner for literature, is now a shrine to the author of such plays as *Sei Personaggi in Cerca d'Autore (Six Characters in Search of an Author)* and *Enrico IV (Henry IV)*. Family photos, paintings, theatrical images, and manuscripts provide an intimate look at the playwright, who is buried under his favorite pine tree.

Contrada Caos, Frazione Caos. ✆ **0922-511826**. Daily 9am–1pm and 2–7pm. Admission 2€. Catch bus no. 1 from Piazza Marconi, just west of the temple zone.

Where to Stay & Eat

Ambasciata di Sicilia ★ SICILIAN   Another reason to venture into modern Agrigento is chance to enjoy a hearty meal at this old-fashioned favorite, a city institution since 1919. True to the name, the kitchen makes it a point to act as Sicilian ambassadors and introduce diners to the island's finest cuisine, specializing in delicious preparations of fresh fish, along with *linguine al'Ambasciata* (prepared with meat sauce, bacon, calamari, and zucchini). Meals are served in a small dining room crammed to the ceiling with marionettes and other colorful artifacts or on a breezy terrace overlooking the rooftops.

Via Gianbertoni 2, off Via Atenea. ✆ **0922-20526.** Main courses 7€–12€. Sept–July Tues–Sun 12:30–3:30pm and

7–11:30pm; Aug daily 12:30–3:30pm and 7–11:30pm. Closed 2 weeks in Nov.

Blu Hotel Kaos ★ The somewhat out of the way location, 2km (1¼ miles) southwest of the Valley of the Temples, is best-suited to travelers with cars, but the garden, pool, sea views, and in-house restaurants make this a good choice for an overnight while making a Sicilian circuit. Despite a resort-like ambiance, the lodgings have some character, fashioned out of a noble residence and two outbuildings.

Contrada Cumbo, Villaggio Pirandello. www.bluhotelkaos.it. ℂ **0922-598622.** 105 units. 74€–99€ double. Free parking. **Amenities:** 3 restaurants; bar; outdoor pool; 2 tennis courts; solarium; babysitting; smoke-free rooms; Wi-Fi (free for first six hrs. of use).

Hotel Villa Athena ★ An 18th-century villa set in gardens within the Valley of the Temples might be the best-located perch in all of Italy. Looking at the Temple of Concord, illuminated at night, is one of Sicily's great travel experiences and can be enjoyed from the

Hotel Villa Athena in Agrigento.

balconies and even the beds of many of the rooms, done with smart traditional furnishings and handsome fabrics. The beautiful garden, surrounding a pool, is also a prime spot to enjoy the view while enjoying a glass of wine.

Via Passeggiata Archeologica 33. www.hotelvillaathena.it. ✆ **0922-596288.** 27 units. 190€–330€ double. Rates include buffet breakfast. Free parking. Bus: 2. **Amenities:** Dining room; 2 bars; outdoor pool; room service; Wi-Fi (free).

SELINUNTE ★★★

122km (76 miles) SW of Palermo

This westernmost Greek colony was one of the most powerful cities in the world, home to 100,000 inhabitants, when the great Carthiginian general Hannibal virtually destroyed it in 409 B.C. He spared only the temples—not out of respect for the deities, but to preserve the loot they housed. Today the vast archaeological park comprises 270 hectares (670 acres), making it Europe's largest archaeological site. Selinunte is not just large, but also beautiful, a bucolic spot where you can walk amid the ruins, gaze out to sea, and ponder what life might have been like millennia ago. As you walk amid the wildflowers and smell the wild herbs, remember that the name of the town name comes from the Greek word *selinon*, meaning parsley.

GETTING THERE   Selinunte is on the southern coast of Sicily and is most easily reached by **car.** From Palermo, take the A29 autostrada and get off at Castelvetrano, following the signs thereafter. Allow about 2 hours for the trip.

From Agrigento, take the scenic Route 115 northwest into Castelvetrano; then follow the sign-posted

The Temple of Segesta.

secondary road marked selinunte, which leads south to the sea.

If you prefer to take the **train** (www.trenitalia.it; ☏ **892021**) from Palermo, you can get off at Castelvetrano, 23km (14 miles) from the ruins. The trip from Palermo to Castelvetrano takes a little over 2 hours (you need to change trains); once at Castelvetrano, board a **bus** for the final lap of the journey to Selinunte. **Autoservizi Salemi** (www.autoservizisalemi.it; ☏ **0923-981120**), which also operates a service from Palermo to Castelvetrano, will take you to the archaeological park in 20 minutes.

Lumia buses (www.autolineelumia.it; ☏ **0922-20414**) run to Castelvetrano station from Agrigento.

VISITOR INFORMATION The tourist office at Via Giovanni Caboto (☏ **0924-46251**), near the archaeological park, is open Monday to Saturday 8am to 2pm and 3 to 8pm, Sunday 9am to noon and 3 to 6pm.

Exploring the Archaeological Park

Given the enormity of the area, allow yourself at least 3 hours to visit, preferably in the early morning. Bring or buy drinks before starting your visit, as you can get rather thirsty under the sun. Ecotour Selinunte runs a hop-on-hop-off service to all the sites within the park on a train of golf carts. For more info, visit www.selinunteservice.com or call ✆ **347-1645862.**

Parco Archeologico Selinunte ★★★ RUINS
The archaeological grounds are designated into three distinct zones: The East Hill and temples, the Acropolis and ancient city, and the Sanctuary of Demeter Malophorus. You will most likely start your visit from the East Hill, adjacent to the main entrance. (Note that archeologists are still trying to determine which deity each of the Doric temples was dedicated to—for now, they are simply denoted by letters of the alphabet.) The **East Hill** was the sacred district of the city, with three temples surrounded by an enclosure. Temple E, which was in all probability dedicated to Hera (Juno), was built between 490 and 480 B.C. and has a staggering 68 columns. The Metopes, the reliefs that are the pride and joy of the archaeological museum in Palermo, are from this temple. Temple F is the oldest of the trio, built between 560 and 540 B.C.; in its original state, it had a double row of 6 columns at the eastern entrance and 14 columns on either side. Temple G, now an impressive heap of rubble except for a lone standing column, was destined to be of colossal proportions if it had been completed in 480 B.C.; even so, it is the second largest temple in Sicily.

Atop a plateau, the **Acropolis,** a district of grid-like streets surrounded by defensive walls, was the center of social and political life. Here stood most of

Selinunte's important public and religious buildings, as well as the residences of the town's aristocrats. Temple C, the earliest surviving temple of ancient Selinus, was built here in the 6th century B.C.; it stands surrounded by 14 of its resurrected 17 columns. From the Acropolis, you cross the now-dry Modione River to the **Sanctuary of Demeter Malophorus,** the ruins of several shrines to Demeter, goddess of fertility. The custom was for worshipers to place stone figurines in the shrines to honor Demeter; as many as 12,000 such figurines have been unearthed.

Parco Archeologico Selinunte. ☏ **0924-46540.** Combined ticket with Parco Archeologico in Segesta (p. 631), valid for 3 days: 9€ adults, 4.50€ ages 18–25, free children 17 and under. Daily 9am to 1 hour before sunset.

Where to Eat

Ristorante Pierrot ★ SICILIAN   The terrace is a perfect place to relax after touring the ruins, and a meal is a introduction to regional cuisine, as typical of North Africa as it is of Italy. Fish couscous is the house specialty, and *orecchiette* and other pastas are laden with swordfish, shrimp, and other seafood that's as fresh as the eggplants and tomatoes right out of the garden that find their way into many dishes and are served as side dishes.

Via Marco Polo 108, Marinella. ☏ **0924-46205.** Main courses 8€–15€. Daily 10am–3pm and 7pm–midnight.

THE WEST COAST

The western stretches of Sicily are a little off the beaten track, but the headlands and peaks are dramatic, the coast is ablaze with the blue sea and white salt pans, and sun-bleached cities show off Arab and North African influences.

ERICE ★★★

96km (60 miles) SW of Palermo, 14km (8⅔ miles) NE of Trapani, 45km (28 miles) NW of Marsala

The enchanting medieval city of Erice, high atop Mount Erice (743m/2,438 ft.), is all about views. On a clear summer's day, you can see west to the Egadi Islands, east to Mount Etna and south to Africa, glimpsing Tunisia's Cape Bon. Views aside, Erice is an impressive place in its own right, with beautifully pre-served medieval squares and palaces that seem a world removed from the rest of the often unruly and ungainly island below. Even the mist that can descend upon Erice in the course of few minutes doesn't diminish the spectacle. Seeing the city's towers and craggy rocks poking through a hazy blanket of gray is a memorable sight in itself.

Essentials

GETTING THERE From Trapani (see p. 140), you have two public transport options. From Piazza Giovanni Paolo II you can take bus no. 21, leaving every 30

PREVIOUS PAGE: **Pepoli castle in Erice.**

minutes and run by **ATM Trapani** (www.atmtrapani. it; ✆ **0923-559575**); pay the fare, (1.20€), on the bus. Get off at the cable-car station is on Via Capua in lower Erice and board the **funivia (cableway)** (www. funiviaerice.it; ✆ **0923-560023**). It will whisk you up to the top in about 10 minutes at a cost of 6€ round-trip (wheelchair accessibility is available). *Note:* The cableway is usually closed on Monday mornings for general maintenance and does not operate in inclement weather; check first before going. You can also make the entire trip by **AST buses** (www.azienda sicilianatrasporti.it; ✆ **840-000323**), departing from Trapani's Piazza Montalto; service is year-round, daily 6:40am to 7:30pm, and the fare is 2.40€. The trip along winding, uphill turns lasts 50 minutes.

Discovering Erice

Erice is an atmospheric place, where you'll stop to per-haps admire an arch, a door, or a bell tower, as you wander its steep cobblestone streets flanked by churches and stone houses with elaborate baroque balconies packed with cascading geraniums. The city is famous throughout Sicily for its pastries, and you'll want to sample such delights as the tangy *dolci di Badia* cakes, made from almond paste and lemon juice.

Whether you come up to Erice by road or cable car, you will arrive at Porta Trapani, one of three entrance gates of the city (the other two are Porta Spada and Porta Spagnola, farther north). The 12th-century Porta Trapani is imbedded in the Elymian-Punic walls, the extensive defensive barrier laid out by the Elymians (the ancient inhabitants of western Sic-ily) around 1200 B.C. and later fortified subsequently by the Carthaginians from North Africa to guard the city from attackers coming from the west.

Steep, cobblestone Via Vittorio Emanuele leads past churches and monasteries to the town high point and central square Piazza Umberto I. From there, Via Guarnotti leads through Piazza San Giuliano to the beautiful Giardino del Balio, surrounding the Norman-era Castello Pepoli. The cliffside promenade beneath the castle affords the most spectacular views in western Sicily, all the way to Tunisia, a distance of 170km (106 miles), on a clear day. The gardens are always open.

Castello di Venere (Castle of Venus) ★ RUIN
The Normans who conquered Sicily in the 12th century built a mountaintop castle, a massive and majestic show of might, on the sight of an ancient temple to Venus. Mammoth medieval towers and the ruins of

The Castle of Venus.

walls still surround the compound, and through defensive slits and other openings you can look out over the plains of Trapani and the Egadi Islands, showing off the sight's defensive advantage. Most intriguing are the rites of the onetime temple, where young women became slaves in a cult to Venus, goddess of love, and serviced male worshippers as part of their duties. This was an honorable profession that ended at the age 21, when the women were set free as desirable brides.

Erice. © **366-6712832**. Admission 3€, 1.50€ children 8–14, free for children 7 and under. Apr–Oct, daily 10am–sunset.

Chiesa Matrice (Royal Duomo of Erice) ★

CHURCH   Rather ironically, Erice's 14th-century Duomo was constructed with stones from the ancient Temple of Venus, that temple of pagan hedonism where young maidens offered their services to supplicants. The campanile (bell tower) that rises 28m (92 ft.) next to the church also has an ancient past, built in the late 15th century atop a watchtower from the 2nd century B.C. Frederick of Aragon, who eventually lost Sicily to the Spanish, ordered construction of the campanile so his sentries could keep an eye out through the medieval mullioned windows for invading troops in the sea lanes far below. The church's porch, dubbed the "Gibbena" (from the Latin *agi bene,* meaning "act well") is a later addition, built to accommodate penitents who were not allowed to partake in the mass. They missed out on worshipping under the vaulted, arabesque ceiling in front of the enormous altarpiece in Carrara marble, depicting the life and times of Christ.

Piazza Umberto I. © **0923-869123**), Admission 2€, free for children 12 and under. Mon–Fri 9:30am–12:30pm and 3:30–5:30pm, Sat–Sun 9:30am–1pm and 3:30–6pm.

Where to Stay & Eat

Hotel Elimo ★   A 400-year-old palazzo in the heart of Erice's historic core welcomes guests in stone-walled lounges where a fire blazes in a hearth beneath beamed ceilings in the chilly months. Guest quarters are a bit more conventional, though comfortable, though some have views over the plains below, as do the restaurant and terrace.

Via Vittorio Emanuele 75. www.hotelelimo.it. ✆ **0923-869377.** 22 units. 110€ double; 185€ suite. **Amenities:** Restaurant; bar; Wi-Fi (free).

Hotel Moderno ★★   The "moderno" dates to the conversion of a 19th-century house just after World War II, though old-fashioned charm prevails. Antiques, brass, and wicker pieces lend a homey touch and about a dozen rooms open onto private balconies or terraces. The view from the terrace, where breakfast can be taken in warm weather, is stunning, and the restaurant is excellent.

Via Vittorio Emanuele 67. www.hotelmodernoerice.it. ✆ **0923-869300.** 40 units. 80€–110€ double. Rates include breakfast. Free parking nearby. **Amenities:** Restaurant; bar; Wi-Fi (free).

Il Carmine ★★   A refurbished 15th-century convent still shows traces of monastic living in simple, no-frills rooms and shower-only bathrooms. Yet the Spartan surroundings are loaded with character, and views into the gardens are as soothing as they were intended to be. There's no curfew, as a separate entrance ensures you won't disturb convent life.

Piazza del Carmine. www.ilcarmine.com. ✆ **0923-1941532.** 6 units. 55€–80€ double. Rates include buffet breakfast. Free parking (except in summer). **Amenities:** Restaurant; Wi-Fi (free).

Where to Eat

Monte San Giuliano ★★★ SICILIAN   You'll navigate some steps and stone alleyways to reach this garden hideaway, where a table on the terrace or in the rustic dining room seems, like much of medieval Erice, far away from the modern world. The menu shows off Arab influences in the flavorful seafood couscous, with many nods to such local favorites as lamb with a pistachio crust and pasta with *sarde* (with sardines) or with *pesto alla Trapanese*, a mix of garlic, basil, fresh tomatoes, and almonds.

Vicolo San Rocco 7. www.montesangiuliano.it. ✆ **0923-869595.** Main courses 8€–15€. Tues–Sun 12:15–2:45pm and 7:30–10pm. Closed Jan 7–21.

PASTRIES

Erice is renowned throughout Sicily for its pastries, refined by cloistered nuns from the 14th to the 18th century. Maria Grammatico, who was raised in the nearby San Carlo convent, became famous in Italy when

Pastries from Pasticceria Grammatico.

she wrote her autobiography, *Bitter Almonds*. Her crunchy almond cookies, rum- or orange-filled marzipan balls, and confections fashioned from chocolate-covered almond paste on offer at **Pasticceria Grammatico** (Via Vittorio Emanuele 14; ✆ 0923-869-390) are a modern legend. **Pasticceria San Carlo** (Via S. Domenico 18, ✆ 0923-869-235) does not enjoy the same celebrity status as Maria Grammatico, but it's just as good and can supply you with a mixed assortment of cookies and other treats to fortify a walk around town.

TRAPANI

100km (62 miles) SW of Palermo, 14km (8⅔ miles) SW of Erice

The big draw along the most westerly stretch of Sicily is the coast from Trapani to Marsala (p. 146), lined with dazzling white salt pans. The flats are protected as a nature reserve populated by migratory birds, and the sight of the vast stretches of white rock salt stretching into the blue horizon broken by red-and-white stone windmills is spectacular. The provincial capital, Trapani, is set below Mount Erice, and the old center on a sea-girt promontory is also quite a sight, an atmospheric maze of medieval streets and squares.

Essentials

GETTING THERE Frequent **trains** from Palermo make the 2½-hour run to Trapani; there are also about a dozen per day from Marsala, taking 30 minutes. Trains pull in at the Piazza Stazione, where luggage storage is available (www.trenitalia.it; ✆ 892021). Terravision (www.terravision.eu; ✆ 0923-981120) operates **bus** service between Palermo and Trapani airport, where you can get a bus into the city center. It's unlikely you'll be arriving by **plane,** though Vincenzo Florio Airport at Birgi, 15km (9 miles) from the center of Trapani (www.airgest.it; ✆ 0923-842502) is the island's third-largest and the main Ryanair hub for Sicily from the U.K. From here, take the buses that connect you to the city or to Palermo. **AST** (www.

aziendasicilianatrasporti.it; ✆ 840-000323) has an hourly service from the airport to Trapani at a cost of 4.50€. From Palermo by **car,** follow the A29 autostrada all the way southwest into Trapani. From Marsala, head north along Route 115 to Trapani.

Trapani is a major embarkation point for **ferries** and **hydrofoils.** Most departures are for the Egadi Islands of Marettimo, Levanzo, and Favignana. Service is also available to Ustica, Pantelleria, Civitavecchia near Rome, and even Tunisia in North Africa. **Ferries** depart from the docks near Piazza Garibaldi. Service is offered by Ustica (www.usticalines.it; ✆ 0923-22200) or Grimaldi (www.grimaldi-lines.com; ✆ 0923-593673).

VISITOR INFORMATION   The **tourist office,** at Via San Francesco d'Assisi (✆ **0923-545511**), is open Monday to Saturday 8am to 8pm, Sunday 9am to noon.

Exploring Trapani

The old town extends westwards out to sea, with a typical North African style and feel in the labyrinth of narrow streets that wind toward the **Torre di Ligny,** built in 1671 on the tip of the peninsula. Many elegant baroque buildings line **Corso Vittorio Emanuele,** sometimes called Rua Grande, as it extends west from the **Palazzo Senatorio,** the 17th-century, pink-marble town hall. Adjacent 18th-century **Via Garibaldi** (also known as Rua Nova, or "New Road") is flanked with palaces and churches. One of them, the 17th-century baroque **Chiesa del Purgatorio,** one block up from Piazza Garibaldi, houses the single greatest treasure in Trapani: The *Misteri,* 20 life-size wooden figures from the 18th century depicting

Trapani's Procession of the Mysteries happens every Good Friday.

Christ's Passion and carried through town for Good Friday's **Processione dei Misteri** (Procession of the Mysteries). The church is open daily 8:30am to 12:30pm and from 4 to 8pm but is often closed. **Via Torrearsa** leads down to a bustling *pescheria* (**fish market**) where tuna is traded; the valuable commodity is caught in nearby waters and traded with buyers from as far away as Japan. **Villa Margherita,** public gardens stretching between old and new Trapani, is an inviting oasis with fountains, banyan trees, and palms rustling in the wind.

Santuario dell'Annunziata/ Museo Regionale Pepoli ★ CHURCH/MUSEUM

The cloisters of a 14th-century convent enclose a collection of archaeological finds and art, many of them salvaged by a local aristocrat, Count Pepoli. With his fine eye the count found the best examples of coral carving, a popular Trapani tradition that local craftspeople pursued well into the early 20th century, when nearby coral beds were depleted. Many of the works, in which coral is often intermingled with silver filigree, are by local artisans Andrea and Alberto Tipa. Among their creations is a spectacularly elaborate *presepe* (nativity scene). Before leaving the premises step into the convent's **Cappella della Madonna** to see a graceful, sculpted scene of the Virgin and Child, attributed to the 14th-century Tuscan master Nino Pisano.

Via Conte Agostino Pepoli 200. ℂ **0923-553269**. Admission 4€, 2€ for children 12 and under. Mon–Sat 9am–1pm and Sun 9am–12:30pm.

Where to Stay

Ligny ★★   Right at the edge of the sea at the end of the Old Town peninsula, each of these high-ceilinged rooms in an old palazzo comes with a panoramic terrace that takes in sweeping views of the gulf and Erice rising above the shores. Beaches, the port, and the town sights are within easy walking distance. Iron bedsteads and some old family pieces add a homey touch to the rooms, up two flights of stairs; bathrooms are shower-only, and some are not en suite. Credit cards are not accepted.

Via Torre Ligny 114. www.ligny.it. ℂ **0923-1941515**. 5 units. 45€–80€ double. Rates include breakfast. Free street parking. **Amenities:** Wi-Fi (free).

Nuovo Albergo Russo ★★   Despite the name, what is just about the oldest hotel in Trapani welcomes guests with solid, old-fashioned comfort and gracious hospitality. Beyond the art-filled lobby, the spotless, plainly furnished rooms are well maintained and comfortable, a nice base from which to explore the streets and squares just outside the door.

Via Tintori 4. nuovorusso.altervista.org. ℂ **0923-22163.** 35 units. 76€–85€ double. Rates include continental breakfast. **Amenities:** Bar; room service; babysitting; Wi-Fi (free).

Where to Eat

Trapani is a good place to try what's considered to be the oldest handmade pasta in the world, *busiati*. The curly, eggless pasta has a firm texture and mealy taste, and is good eaten with pesto sauce made Trapanese style with cherry tomatoes.

Ai Lumi Tavernetta ★ SICILIAN   The narrow, arched, ground floor of a palazzo, filled with heavy rustic tables and chairs, is a cool retreat in which to enjoy Trapanese classics. Seafood is plentiful, as are such meat specialties as roast lamb in a citrus sauce and busiati, the thick local pasta that seems like perfection itself when simply topped with tomato, basil, and pecorino. The terrace in front is one of the nicest places in Trapani to spend a summer evening.
Corso Vittorio Emanuele 75. www.ailumi.it. ✆ **0923-872418.** Main courses 8€–18€. Sept–July Mon–Sat 7:30–11pm; Aug daily 7:30–11pm.

Osteria La Bettolaccia ★★ SICILIAN   Trapani's longtime favorite never disappoints, drawing big crowds (reserve if you can) to a couple of rambling, tile-floored rooms near the seafront. The kitchen prepares what many regulars claim is the best seafood couscous in Sicily, laden with calamari and a spicy sauce. Another favorite is spaghetti with swordfish, tuna, tomatoes, herbs, and breadcrumbs.
25 Via Enrico Fardella. ✆ **0923-21695.** Main courses 8€–15€. Mon–Fri 1–3pm and 7–11pm, Sat 1–3pm.

Around Trapani

Trapani is wedged between two especially scenic stretches of coastline. To the northeast is the dramatic headland at San Vito Lo Capo, with fine beaches and the Zingaro nature reserve. Stretching south of Trapani are coastal salt pans that have been harvested since antiquity.

RISERVA NATURALE DELLO ZINGARO & SAN VITO LO CAPO

The most beautiful stretch of coastline in Sicily extends 12km/7½ miles north from the tiny town of Scopello (35km/21 miles) east of Trapani to the headland of San Vito Lo Capo. The beaches can be impossibly crowded in summer, but they're paradisiacal, much like those in the Caribbean. The alternating sand and pebble shores are etched with coves. The **Tonnara di Scopello,** at the edge of Scopello, is an especially idyllic spot to swim. The abandoned 13th-century tuna-processing plant is surrounded by wind-shaped rocks and faces a sparkling cove. Much of the land is set aside as the **Riserva Naturale dello Zingaro** (www.riservazingaro.it; ✆ 092-435108), the first designated wildlife area in Sicily and covering nearly 1,600 hectares (3,954 acres) of Mediterranean maquis and coastline. Within the reserve is also the **Grotta dell'Uzzo,** a cave that served as a dwelling place in Paleolithic times, and now is a refuge for six different types of bats (off limits to all but sanctioned naturalists). Motorized vehicles are prohibited (the only transport is by mule).

THE SALT MARSHES ★★★

Stretching from Trapani to Marsala along route SP21, the salt pans along the coast have been harvested since antiquity. For millennia, salt was used as a preservative for perishable food and for the Romans was compensation for mercenaries (the word "salary" derives from the Latin *salaries* meaning "soldier's

Harvested salt.

allowance for the purchase of salt"). The area has now been protected as the **Riserva Naturale Orientata "Saline di Trapani e Paceco"** (www.wwfsaline ditrapani.it; ✆ 0923-867700), covering 1,000 hectares (2,471 acres). If possible, visit in the late afternoon, when you'll witness sunsets against a terse evening sky that changes color as the sun goes down and as the migrating birds perform their spectacular in-flight choreographies.

MARSALA

31km (19 miles) S of Trapani, 124km (77 miles) SW of Palermo

This thriving little port on Cape Boéo, the western-most tip of Sicily overlooking the Egadi Islands and Tunisia, is where the world-famous Marsala sweet wine is produced. You can drink some of the amber yellow Marsala in one of the town's quaint wine shops,

Salt of the Earth

When the Carthaginians first landed in the area from North Africa they saw the potential for salt production and conditions and created basins from which to harvest the valuable commodity. The process exploits the high level of salinity in the seawater and the wind and sun that contribute to the evaporation process. Water is pumped in mid to late winter into the pans through a canal. Over the next few months the water is left to evaporate, when it assumes a reddish color dense with mineral pigment. Around July, just as the water reaches a sluggish consistency, the salt is raked and harvested, and brought onto dry land to complete the exsiccation process. What look like little salt huts line the road, covered in terra-cotta tiles to protect them from the elements. Once completely dry, the salt is cleansed of debris and packaged.

or head through the hills along roads lined with prickly-pear cacti to one of the vineyards nearby. Townspeople sip the dark, vintage Marsala as a dessert wine with hard piquant cheese, fruit or pastries. Famous product aside, Marsala is an elegant town with baroque palaces and churches, Roman ruins, a lively fish market, and a long sandy coastline stretching to the north and south.

Essentials

GETTING THERE   **Trains** (www.trenitalia.it; ☎ **892021**) run daily between Marsala and Trapani and Palermo. The journey takes 30 minutes from Trapani, up to 3½ hours from Palermo. AST **Buses** (www.aziendasiciliana trasporti.it; ☎ **0923-21021**) for Marsala leave from Piazza Montalto in Trapani at the rate of three per day. The one-way trip lasts 35 minutes. From Palermo,

Salemi (www.autoservizisalemi.it; © **0923 981120;**) runs several buses to the town center. The journey takes 1 hour 45 minutes. By **car,** head south from Trapani along Route 115.

VISITOR INFORMATION The **tourist office,** at Via 11 Maggio 100 (© **0923-714097**), is open Monday to Saturday 8am to 1:45pm and 2 to 8pm, Sunday 9am to noon.

What to See & Do

Enter the city from the **Porta Garibaldi,** a glorious gateway from the 1600s crowned by an eagle. Garibaldi is honored because it was at Marsala that the 19th-century freedom fighter and his red-shirted volunteers overthrew the Bourbon regime, paving the way for the independence of southern Italy. The road from the gate leads on to **Via Garibaldi,** where it ends at the busy **Piazza della Repubblica,** the heart of the city. The square's **Palazzo Senatorio,** now the Town Hall, dates from the 18th century and is nicknamed

A vineyard growing the famed grapes of the region.

"Loggia." Leading north from Piazza Repubblica is the main thoroughfare, **Via 11 Maggio**, flanked by the town's most splendid baroque palaces. To the northwest, facing the sea on the **Lungomare Boéo,** the archaeological museum (see below) stands amid many old *bagli*, or Marsala wine warehouses. A little farther along are the excavations of the ancient Lilybaeum or the **Insula Romana,** an archaeological area open to the public 24 hours a day. It contains the remains of a Roman villa, true to Marsala's imperial past, (which had a steam room, among its other trappings), and well-preserved mosaics.

Chiesa Madre ★ CHURCH   It's only fitting that Marsala's most imposing church is dedicated to British saint St. Thomas à Becket, given the English connections that brought the city such wealth over the centuries (see box). Legend has it that a ship carrying materials to build a church dedicated to the saint was on its way to England when a storm forced it to seek shelter in the harbor of Marsala. It's more likely that the cult-like popularity of the saint, murdered in Canterbury cathedral in 1170, had spread to Sicily when the church was founded in the 13th century. The most impressive decorative pieces in the three-aisle interior are also by outsiders, the 15th-century Gaginis. The family of sculptors worked their way from their native Switzerland down the Italian boot until they undertook commissions in Palermo and elsewhere around Sicily. Here their best work, by Domenico Gagini, is lovely *Madonna del Popolo* in the right transept.

Piazza della Repubblica. ✆ **0923-716295.** Free admission. Daily 7:30am to 7pm.

Museo Archaeologico Nave Punica–Baglio Anselmi ★★ MUSEUM

A former wine warehouse (*baglio*) houses gold jewelry from ancient Mozia (see p. 153) while the showpiece is a well-preserved **Punic ship** (Punic being the Latin name for Carthage, the ancient kingdom in what is today's Tunisia). It's believed the ship, discovered in shallow waters in 1971, was constructed for the Battle of the Egadi Islands during the First Punic Wars between the Romans and Carthaginians in 241 B.C. and sank on its maiden voyage; some scholars argue that the vessel was not a warship but was used to carry cargo. Measuring 35m (115 ft.) long, the ship was manned by 68 oarsmen. Large sections remain, enough to suggest the sleekness and power of the wooden shell covered with sheets of lead fixed with bronze nails. They are on display along with bowls, plates, animal bones, cannabis leaves, and other material carried on board.

Lungomare Boéo. ☏ **0923-952535**. Admission 4€ adults, 2€ children 17 and under. Wed–Sat 9am–7pm, Sun–Tues 9am–1pm.

Museo degli Arazzi (Tapestry Museum) ★★ MUSEUM

Eight Flemish tapestries, made in Brussels between 1530 and 1550, are the legacy of a bishop of Messina, who donated them to his hometown of Marsala. Tucked away for centuries, and at one point almost auctioned off, the exquisite silk and wool pieces once hung in the royal palace in Madrid. They depict scenes from the Roman wars against the Jews from A.D. 66 to A.D. 67, when troops of Flavius Vespasian occupied Jerusalem. The tapestries are kept in darkened rooms to avoid damage.

Via Garraffa 57. ☏ **0923-711327**. Admission 2.50€. Mon–Sat 9am–1pm and 4–6pm, Sun 9am–1pm.

THE wine THAT PUT MARSALA ON THE MAP

On a dark and stormy night in 1770, English trader John Woodhouse was forced to anchor in Marsala during a violent storm. He headed for a tavern, downed some local wine, discovered it tasted similar to the Portuguese "Porto," and realized it had commercial potential. Woodhouse began to mass-produce and export the wine. He got a big break when the legendary Admiral Horatio Nelson developed a taste for the wine and decided the British Navy should allot sailors a glass per day.

Around the same time, Joseph Whitaker, another young English entrepreneur, inherited a vast vineyard in Marsala and further expanded the wine's reputation by exporting it to the United States. He also bought the island of Mozia (p. 153), where he founded an archaeological museum and published important studies of Tunisian birds.

One more enterprising businessman entered the scene when Vincenzo Florio, from Palermo, purchased the Woodhouse wine empire in the mid-19th century and refined Marsala grapes. The Florio clan also exported tuna and was one of Sicily's most prominent families well into the 20th century.

A place to sample Marsala is **Enoteca La Ruota** on Lungomare Boéo near the archeological museum (number 36/A, ✆ **0923-715241**). You can sip the local wines while admiring the Stagnone lagoon lying in front of you.

Where to Stay & Eat

New Hotel Palace ★   The 19th-century estate of an English wine importer has been redone and added onto, but the premises retain a luxurious, old-world aura. The most desirable rooms are in the old house, but those in the new annex are well done, too, and all are spacious and stylishly decorated with traditional furnishings; many have sea views. In the surrounding gardens, stately old trees are a backdrop for the swimming pool.

Lungomare Mediterraneo 57. www.newhotelpalace.com. ☎ **0923-719492.** 56 units. 95€–130€ double. Rates include buffet breakfast. Free parking. **Amenities:** Restaurant; bar; outdoor pool; room service; babysitting; Wi-Fi (free).

Villa Favorita ★★

An early 19th-century hunting lodge is a rather exotic retreat, tucked into lush gardens at the edge of historic Marsala. Guest quarters are spread between the elegant villa, with wide-oak and tile floors and arched loggias opening onto a courtyard, and garden bungalows. All the accommodations are spacious, with plain but tasteful furnishings, and they surround a beautiful swimming pool and many quite, shaded corners. The restaurant serves well-done Sicilian dishes.

Via Favorita 23. www.villafavorita.com. ☎ **0923-989100.** 29 bungalows, 13 units in the main building. 85€– 125€ double. Rates include buffet breakfast. Free parking. From the center of Marsala, take the SS115 toward Trapani. The hotel is signposted. **Amenities:** Restaurant; bar; outdoor pool; tennis court; Wi-Fi (free).

Trattoria Garibaldi ★ SICILIAN/SEAFOOD

At this 50-year-old favorite near the cathedral, four arched, colorful dining rooms serve local favorites with a well-deserved reputation for freshness. Seafood, whether simply grilled with spices or served atop couscous, has a decidedly North African flare, while *busiate* (the local homemade pasta) served with fresh fish is specialty you probably won't encounter beyond the west coast.

Piazza dell'Addolorata 35. www.trattoriagaribaldi.com. ☎ **0923-953006.** Main courses 7€–13€. Mon–Fri noon–3pm and 7:30–10pm; Sat 7:30–10pm; Sun noon–3pm.

Around Marsala

MOZIA ★★★

2km (1 mile) W of Marsala, 15 km (9 miles) SW of Trapani.

The tiny island of San Pantaleo in the Stagnone, a lagoon and nature reserve, is littered with the ruins of the ancient city of Motya (today's Mozia). The island, owned by the Whitakers, Marsala's winemaking family, is also a wonderful place to observe the pink flamingoes, curlews, and egrets that visit the lagoon. In summer the sparse landscape is abloom with white sea daffodil and sea lavender. **Arini and Pugliese ferries** (www. arinipugliese.com; ☎ **347-7790218**) runs a daily, year-round service to Mozia from Marsala and costs 5€ return, 2.50€ for schoolchildren and adults 65 and over.

Mozia was a stronghold of the Phoenicians, who eventually migrated to Carthage (present-day Tunisia), and by the 6th century B.C. the island settlement was surrounded by nearly 2.5km (1½ miles) of defensive walls. In 397 B.C., Dionysius the Elder of Syracuse mounted a massive attack on the inhabitants, who retreated to Lilybaeum (now Marsala).

Footpaths meander through the scattered ruins, and the free island map (available at the boat landing) is essential in making sense of what can seem like not much more than the ruins of low walls here and there. Most intact are the **Casa dei Mosaici (House of Mosaics),** with scenes from animal life dating to the 4th to 3rd century B.C., and the Tophet, a Phoenician burial ground for victims of child sacrifice, where the gravestones, *stele*, are intricately carved. The best of the artifacts to have been excavated on the island are in the **Villa Malfitano** museum. The prize is a sensual marble statue of a young man in a wet tunic, the **Giovane di Mozia (Young Man of Mozia),** which dates to around 440 B.C.

EGADI ISLANDS

9km (15 miles) NW of Marsala, 10km (16 miles) SW of Trapani

An archipelago of three islands (Favignana, Levanzo, and Marettimo) forms the westernmost point of Sicily and is a place to get away from it all. The islands are popular summertime retreats for swimming and scuba-diving, but the rest of the year their 4,600 inhabitants are left to live from the fruits of the sea, as they have done for centuries.

A beach in Favignana.

Each of the islands has a distinct character, and it's possible to take in Roman ruins, Paleolithic and Neolithic cave paintings, grottoes, and natural springs. None of the islands is large, two are free of cars, and their deserted mountain paths make them attractive spots for walking.

The islands are home to the largest tuna fishery in Sicily, and famous for the annual *mattanza,* an age-old method of culling tuna (p. 156).

Essentials

GETTING THERE **Ustica Lines** (www.usticalines.it; ✆ **0923-873813**) runs a daily ferry and hydrofoil service almost every hour from Trapani and Marsala to Favignana, Levanzo, and Marettimo.

What to See & Do

The island sought out by most vacationers, **Favignana** presents two distinct landscapes: Flat pastures to the east and desolate crags to the west. The best swimming is at the rocky bay at **Cala Rossa**, while other beaches are between **Grotta Pergiata** and **Punta Longa**. In the middle of it all is Favignana proper, built in 1637. Numerous tuna-canning facilities, many abandoned, are evidence of a thriving business on the island, and many of the shops here sell the local specialty, *bottarga,* or dried tuna roe. Favignana isn't immune to building speculation, and sadly, many new edifices are built over prehistoric ruins.

Levanzo, the smallest island of the archipelago, is also the richest historically, as the first traces of human settlements in Sicily dating back to the Paleolithic times have been found in the **Grotta del**

A gory **SPECTACLE**

La Mattanza, the millennia-old method of catching tuna, draws crowds to the Egadi Islands from all over the world in May and June. Local fishermen, overseen by the *Rais* (leader), head out to the waters to catch the tuna that have come to breed in the deep waters between the islands of Favignana and Levanzo. Nets are placed in the water to form a corridor through which the fish are forced to swim into the *camera della morte*, or chamber of death. Packed together, the tuna wound and stun each other in an attempt to make an escape. When the Rais deems that enough fish have been caught, he orders the hauling in of the nets—an arduous task done in synchronized movements kept in time by the chanting of ancient fishermen songs. Once pulled to the surface, the tuna are harpooned and pulled on board and the sea becomes ruby red. Not surprisingly, several animal protection organizations are demanding that this sort of fishing be banned.

Genovese. The cave is reached by an exhausting 2-hour hike or by boat, though you won't be able to see much: It is now closed to the public after vandals damaged some of the graffiti. Known to Pliny the Elder as *Bucinna,* the island has no natural water reserves, but also no cars, and with its patches of maquis of fragrant plants and cobalt blue seas it can seem like a remote paradise.

Marettimo, the remotest of the islands, is also a Crusoe's paradise—it's been suggested that in the *Odyssey* this might have been the island of Ithaca, the home to which the wandering Odysseus struggles to return. Known as the ancient Hieromesus, the island has no cars and no hotels, and is without a doubt the most beautiful of the three. It is home to many rare species of plants and the occasional wild boar and *mouflon* (wild sheep). They thrive amid natural springs, grottoes, and limestone pinnacles on the flanks of **Monte Falcone** (686m/2,250 ft.). In the tiny village of **Marettimo** proper there are some Roman ruins and a Paleochristian church. Interestingly, what few inhabitants there were on the island at the beginning of the 1900s immigrated to Monterey, California, bringing the art of tuna canning with them. Their story is immortalized in John Steinbeck's novel *Cannery Row*.

Where to Stay & Eat

All of the islands are great places to eat fish, and what's been caught that day is what's served. Couscous with poached fish and tuna simmered in a pot with tomatoes, capers, anchovies, and herbs are island favorites.

Bouganville ★ Beaches, the ferry, and island countryside are all within easy walk of this pretty house in the center of Favignana town. Rooms are fairly no-frills, but they're spacious and have high ceilings and a lot of simple Mediterranean charm. Breakfast is served on a terrace, and another patio is set up for relaxing. The restaurant is an island favorite, with outdoor dining in warmer months.

Via Cimabue 10, Favignana. www.albergobouganville.it. ✆ **0923-22033.** 13 units. 100€–140€ double. Rates include breakfast. Free parking. **Amenities:** Restaurant; bar; Wi-Fi (in lobby, free).

Paradiso ★ The beach is within walking distance, and all of the spacious, no-frills rooms have a sea-facing terrace—an amenity that may well compensate for the Spartan surroundings. So does the restaurant, where you will enjoy your fill of fresh seafood on a pleasant terrace that overlooks the beach.

Via Lungomare, Levanzo www.isoladilevanzo.it. © **0923-924083.** 15 units. 120€–180€ double, with half-board. **Amenities:** Restaurant; bar; Wi-Fi (free). Closed Nov–May.

PLANNING YOUR TRIP TO SICILY

Sicily is loaded with "must see" cities and sights, and most of us have limited vacation time. You want to get there efficiently, get around by road or rail without hassle, and spend as much time soaking up the atmosphere of *Bella Italia* as you can. This chapter shows you how. It may be a long way from home, but when you get there Sicily need not be expensive: Below you'll find advice on where and how to shave travel costs without trimming your fun.

GETTING THERE
By Plane

If you're flying across an ocean, you'll most likely land at Rome's **Leonardo da Vinci–Fiumicino Airport** (FCO; www.adr.it/fiumicino), 40km (25 miles) from the center, or **Milan Malpensa** (MXP; www.milano malpensa-airport.com), 45km (28 miles) northwest of central Milan. Rome's much smaller **Ciampino Airport** (CIA; www.adr.it/ciampino) serves low-cost airlines connecting to European cities and other destinations in Italy. It's the same story with Milan's **Linate Airport** (LIN; www.milanolinate-airport.com).

FLYING DIRECTLY TO PALERMO
From Milan, **easyJet** (www.easyjet.com) and **Alitalia** (www.alitalia.com) connect Milan's Malpensa Airport

with both Palermo and Catania in Sicily. **Meridiana** (www.meridiana.it) flies Milan Linate to Catania. **Ryanair** (www.ryanair.com) connects Bergamo with Palermo, Trapani, and Catania. Direct **Rome** to Sicily routes are operated by Alitalia, Meridiana, and Ryanair. Alitalia, **Volotea** (www.volotea.com), and **Air One** (www.flyairone.com) operate direct flights between **Venice** and Palermo. Volotea and Air One also fly from Venice or Verona to Catania, and from Verona or Turin to Palermo. Air One flies to Catania from Pisa. Volotea also connects Catania with Genoa, as well as Palermo with Genoa, Bari, and Naples. EasyJet links Naples and Catania.

For information on arriving in Sicily via Palermo's airport, see p. 20.

Begin thinking about flying plans at least 6 months ahead of time. Consider exchange rate movements: Fares may be calculated in US dollars or euros, depending on the airline. The key window for finding a **deal** is usually between 5 and 6 months ahead of your departure according to a massive study of some 21 million fare transactions by the Airline Reporting Corporation (a middleman between travel agencies and the airlines). They also found that those who booked on a Sunday statistically found the best rates (on average they paid 19% less than those who booked midweek). Run searches through the regular online agents such as Expedia, as well as metasearch engines like **DoHop.com, Kayak.com, Skyscanner.net,** and **Momondo.com**. For complex journeys, with multiple departures, doing multiple searches (so affordable intra-European airlines such as Germanwings, EasyJet and Ryanair show up on the search) is a good way to find deals; a specialist flight agent such as **RoundtheWorldFlights.com** or **AirTreks.com** will also likely save you money.

GETTING AROUND
By Car

Much of Sicily is accessible by public transportation, but to explore outlying sights, countryside, and smaller towns, a car will save you time. You'll get the **best rental rate** if you book your car far ahead of arrival. Try such websites as **Kayak.com**, **CarRentals.co.uk**, **Skyscanner.net,** and **Momondo.com** to compare prices across multiple rental companies and agents. Car rental search companies usually report the lowest rates being available between 6 and 8 weeks ahead of arrival. Rent the smallest car possible to minimize fuel costs.

You must be 25 or older to rent from many agencies (although some accept ages 21 and up, at a premium price).

The legalities and contractual obligations of renting a car in Italy (where accident rates are high) are more complicated than those in almost any other country in Europe. You also must have nerves of steel, a sense of humor, and a valid driver's license or **International Driver's Permit.** Insurance on all vehicles is compulsory.

Note: If you're planning to rent a car in Sicily during high season, you should **book well in advance.** If you're planning on beginning your trip in Palermo, by all means wait until you are moving on to rent your car. The city is no place for the uninitiated to drive, street parking is risky, and garages are expensive.

Before leaving home, you can apply for an **International Driving Permit** from the American Automobile Association (www.aaa.com; ℂ **800/622-7070** or 650/294-7400). In Canada, the permit's available from the Canadian Automobile Association (www.caa.ca; ✆ **416/221-4300**). Technically, you need this permit and your actual driver's license to drive in Italy, though in practice your license itself often suffices. Visitors from within the EU need only take their domestic driver's license.

Italy's equivalent of AAA is the **Automobile Club d'Italia (ACI**; www.aci.it). They're the people who respond when you place an emergency call to ✆ **803-116** (✆ 800-116-800 from a non-Italian cellphone) for road breakdowns, though they do charge for this service if you're not a member.

DRIVING RULES Italian drivers aren't maniacs; they only appear to be. Spend any time on a highway and you will have the experience of somebody driving up insanely close from behind, headlights flashing. Take a deep breath and don't panic: This is the aggressive signal for you to move to the right so he (invariably, it's a "he") can pass, and until you do he will stay mind-bogglingly close. On a two-lane road, the idiot passing someone in the opposing traffic who has swerved into your lane expects you to veer obligingly over toward the shoulder so three lanes of traffic can fit—he would do the same for you. Probably. Many Italians seem to think that blinkers are optional, so be aware that the car in front could be getting ready to turn at any moment.

Autostrade are toll highways, denoted by green signs and a number prefaced with an *A*. A few fast highways aren't numbered and are simply called a *raccordo,* a connecting road between two cities (such as Florence–Siena and Florence–Pisa).

Strade statali (singular is *strada statale*) are state roads, sometimes without a center divider and two lanes wide (although sometimes they can be a divided four-way highway), indicated by blue signs. Their route numbers are prefaced with an SS, as in the SS11 from Milan to Venice. On signs, however, these official route numbers are used infrequently. Usually, you'll just see blue signs listing destinations by name with arrows pointing off in the appropriate directions. The *strade statali* can be frustratingly slow due to traffic, traffic lights, and the fact that they bisect countless towns: When available, pay for the autostrada.

The **speed limit** on roads in built-up areas around towns and cities is 50 kmph (31 mph). On two-lane roads it's 90 kmph (56 mph) and on the highway its 130 kmph (81 mph). Italians have an astounding disregard for these limits. However, police can ticket you and collect the fine on the spot. The blood-alcohol limit in Italy is .05%, often achieved with just two small drinks; driving above the limit can result in a fine of up to 6,000€, a driving ban, or imprisonment. The blood-alcohol limit is set at zero for anyone who has held a driver's license for under 3 years.

Safety belts are obligatory in both the front and the back seats; ditto child seats or special restraints for minors under 1.5 meters (5 ft.) in height, though this latter regulation is often ignored. Drivers may not use a handheld cellphone while driving—yet another law that locals seem to consider optional.

PARKING On streets, **white lines** indicate free public spaces, **blue lines** are pay public spaces, and **yellow lines** mean only residents are allowed to park. Meters don't line the sidewalk; rather, there's one machine on the block where you punch in coins corresponding to how long you want to park. The machine spits out a ticket that you leave on your dashboard.

If you park in an area marked *parcheggio disco orario*, root around in your rental car's glove compartment for a cardboard parking disc (or buy one at a gas station). With this device, you dial up the hour of your arrival and display it on your dashboard. You're allowed *un'ora* (1 hr.) or *due ore* (2 hr.), according to the sign. If you do not have a disk, write your arrival time clearly on a sheet of paper and leave it on the dash.

Parking lots have ticket dispensers, but exit booths are not usually manned. When you return to the lot to depart, first visit the office or automated payment machine to exchange your ticket for a paid receipt or token, which you will then use to get through the exit gate.

ROAD SIGNS A **speed limit** sign is a black number inside a red circle on a white background. The **end of a speed zone** is just black and white, with a black slash through the number. A red circle with a white background, a black arrow pointing down, and a red arrow pointing up means **yield to oncoming traffic,** while a point-down red-and-white triangle means **yield ahead.**

Many city centers are closed to traffic and a simple white circle with a red border, or the words *zona pedonale* or *zona traffico limitato,* denotes a **pedestrian zone** (you can sometimes drive through to drop off baggage at your hotel); a white arrow on a blue background is used for Italy's many **one-way streets;** a mostly red circle with a horizontal white slash means **do not enter.** Any image in black on a white background surrounded by a red circle means that image is

not allowed (for instance, if the image is two cars next to each other, it means no passing; a motorcycle means no Harleys permitted; and so on). A circular sign in blue with a red circle-slash means **no parking.**

Gasoline (gas or petrol), *benzina,* can be found in pull-in gas stations along major roads and on the outskirts of town, as well as in 24-hour stations along the autostrada. Almost all stations are closed for the *riposo* and on Sundays (except for those on the autostrade), but the majority of them have a machine that accepts cash. Unleaded gas is *senza piombo.* Diesel is *gasolio.*

When buying a regular ticket, ask for either *andata* (one-way) or *andata e ritorno* (round-trip). The best way to avoid presenting yourself on the train with the wrong ticket is to tell the person at the ticket window exactly what train you are going to take, for example, "the 11:30am train for Venice." Regular R or RV tickets are not valid on high-speed trains.

If you don't have a ticket with a reservation for a particular seat on a specific train, then you must **validate you ticket by stamping it in the little yellow box** on the platform before boarding the train. If you board a train without a ticket, or without having validated your ticket, you'll have to pay a hefty fine on top of the ticket or supplement, which the conductor will sell you. If you knowingly board a train without a ticket or realize once onboard that you have the wrong type of ticket, your best bet is to search out the conductor, who is likely to be more forgiving because you found him and made it clear you weren't trying to ride for free.

Schedules for all trains leaving a given station are printed on yellow posters tacked up on the station wall (a similar white poster lists all the arrivals). These are good for getting general guidance, but keep your eye on the electronic boards and television screens that are updated with delays and track (*binario*) changes. You can also get official schedules (plus more train information, also in English) and buy tickets at both www.trenitalia.com and **www.italotreno.it**.

By Bus

You can get just about anywhere on a network of local, provincial, and regional bus lines. Keep in mind that in smaller towns, buses exist mainly to shuttle workers and schoolchildren, so the most runs are on weekdays, early in the morning, and usually again in midafternoon.

Bus stops are usually either in the main square, on the edge of town, or the bend in the road just outside the main town gate. You'll also find them near the main train station in Palermo and Catania. You should always try to find the local ticket vendor—if there's no office, it's invariably the nearest newsstand or *tabacchi* (signaled by a sign with a white T), or occasionally a bar—but you can usually also buy tickets on the bus. You can sometimes flag down a bus as it passes on a country road, but try to find an official stop (a small sign tacked onto a telephone pole). Tell the driver where you're going and ask him courteously if he'll let you know when you need to get off. When he says, "*È la prossima fermata,*" that means yours is the next stop. "*Posso scendere a...?*" (*Poh*-so *shen*-dair-ay ah...?) is "Can I get off at...?"

[FastFACTS] ITALY

Area Codes   The **country code** for Italy is **39.** Some codes for cities in Sicily are 011 (Palermo), 0931 (Siracusa) and 0923 (Trapani). You must dial the entire number, ***including the initial zero,*** when calling from *anywhere* outside or inside Italy and even within the same town. For example, to call Palermo from the United States, you must dial **011-39-01,** then the local phone number. Phone numbers in Italy can range anywhere from 6 to 12 digits in length.

ATMs   The easiest and best way to get cash away from home is from an ATM (automated teller machine), referred to in Italy as a ***bancomat.*** ATMs are prevalent in Italian cities and while every town usually has one, it's good practice to fuel up on cash in urban centers before traveling to villages or rural areas.

Be sure to confirm with your bank that your card is valid for international withdrawal and that you have a four-digit PIN. (Some ATMs in Italy will not accept any other number of digits.) Also, be sure you know your daily withdrawal limit before you depart. ***Note:*** Many banks impose a fee every time you use a card at another bank's ATM, and that fee can be higher for international transactions (up to $5 or more) than for domestic ones. In addition, the bank from which you withdraw cash may charge its own fee, although this is not common practice in Italy.

Business Hours   General open hours for **stores, offices,** and **churches** are from 9:30am to noon or 1pm and again from 3 or 3:30pm to 7:30 or 8pm. The early afternoon shutdown is the *riposo,* the Italian siesta. Most stores close all day Sunday and many also on Monday (morning only or all day). Some services and business offices are open to the public only in the morning. **Banks** tend to be open Monday through Friday 8:30am to 1:30pm and 2:45 to 4:15pm. Traditionally, **state museums** are closed Mondays. Most of the large museums stay open all day long otherwise, although some close for *riposo* or are only open in the morning (9am–2pm is popular). Some churches open earlier in the morning, and the largest often stay open all day, though the last hour or so of opening is usually taken up with an evening service, during which tourist visits are frowned upon.

Customs   Foreign visitors can bring along most items for personal use duty-free, including merchandise valued up to $800.

Disabled Travelers   A few of the top museums and churches have installed ramps at their entrances, and several hotels have converted first-floor rooms into accessible units. Other than that, you may not find parts of Sicily easy to tackle. Builders in the Middle Ages and the Renaissance didn't have wheelchairs or mobility impairments in mind when they built narrow doorways and spiral staircases, and preservation laws prevent Italians from doing much about this in some areas.

Some buses and trains can cause problems as well, with high, narrow doors and steep steps at entrances—though the situation on public transportation, especially the railways, is improving. For those with disabilities who can make it onto buses and trains, there are usually seats reserved for them, and Italians are quick to give up their space for somebody who looks like they need it more than them.

Accessible Italy (www.accessibleitaly.com; ✆ **378-0549-941-111**) provides travelers with info about accessible tourist sites and places to rent wheelchairs, and also sells organized "Accessible Tours" around Italy. Disabled travelers should call **Trenitalia** (✆ **199-303060**) for assistance on the state rail network. Italo has a couple of dedicated wheelchair spaces on every service: Call ✆ **06-07-08.**

Drinking Laws   People of any age can legally consume alcohol in Italy, but a person must be 16 years old in order to be served alcohol in a restaurant or a bar. Noise is the primary concern to city officials, and so bars generally close around 2am, though alcohol is commonly served in clubs after that. Supermarkets carry beer, wine, and spirits.

Electricity   Italy operates on a 220-volt AC (50 cycles) system, as opposed to the U.S. 110-volt AC (60 cycles) system. You'll need a simple adapter plug to make the American flat pegs fit the Italian round holes and, unless your appliance is dual-voltage (as some hair dryers, travel irons, and almost all laptops are), an electrical currency converter. You can pick up the hardware at electronics stores, luggage shops, and airports.

Embassies & Consulates   A U.S. Consular Office is in Palermo at Via Vaccarini 1; http://naples.usconsulate.gov,

① 091-305807. Services are limited, though you should contact the office in emergencies and with questions. The **U.K. Embassy** (www. gov.uk/government/world/italy.it; ① **06-4220-0001**) is in Rome at Via XX Settembre 80a.

Emergencies   The best number to call in Italy (and the rest of Europe) with a **general emergency** is ① **112,** which connects you to the *carabinieri* who will transfer your call as needed. For the **police,** dial ① **113;** for a **medical emergency** and to call an **ambulance,** the number is ① **118;** for the **fire department,** call ① **115.** If your car breaks down, dial ① **116** for **roadside aid** courtesy of the Automotive Club of Italy. All are free calls, but roadside assistance is a paid-for service for nonmembers.

Family Travel   Italy is a family-oriented society. A crying baby at a dinner table is greeted with a knowing smile rather than with a stern look. Children almost always receive discounts, and maybe a special treat from the waiter, but the availability of such accoutrements as child seats for cars and dinner tables is more the exception than the norm. (The former, however, is a legal requirement: Be sure to ask a rental car company to provide one.) There are plenty of parks, offbeat museums, markets, ice-cream parlors, and vibrant street-life scenes to amuse even the youngest children. Child discounts apply on public transportation, and at public and private museums.

Health   You won't encounter any special health risks by visiting Sicily. The country's public health care system is generally well regarded.

Italy offers universal health care to its citizens and those of other European Union countries (U.K. nationals should remember to carry an EHIC: See **www.nhs.uk/ehic**). Others should be prepared to pay medical bills upfront. Before leaving home, find out what medical services your **health insurance** covers. **Note:** Even if you don't have insurance, you will always be treated in an emergency room.

Pharmacies offer essentially the same range of generic drugs available in the United States and internationally. Pharmacies are ubiquitous (look for the green cross) and serve almost like miniclinics, where pharmacists diagnose and treat minor ailments, like flu symptoms and general aches and pains, with over-the-counter drugs. Carry the generic name of any prescription medicines you take, in case a local pharmacist is unfamiliar with the brand name. Pharmacies in cities take turns doing the night shift; normally there is a list posted at the entrance of each pharmacy informing customers which pharmacy is open each night of the week.

Insurance   Italy may be one of the safer places you can travel in the world, but accidents and setbacks can and do happen, from lost luggage to car crashes. For information on traveler's insurance, trip cancellation insurance, and medical insurance while traveling, please visit **www.frommers.com/tips**.

Internet Access   Internet cafes are in healthy supply in most Sicilian cities, though don't expect to find them in every small town. If you're traveling with your own computer or smartphone, you'll find wireless access in almost every hotel, but if this is essential for your stay make sure you ask before booking and certainly don't always expect to find a connection in a rural *agriturismo* (disconnecting from the 21st century is part of their appeal). In a pinch, hostels, local libraries, and some bars will have some sort of terminal for access. Take your passport or other photo ID when you go looking for an Internet point.

LGBT Travelers   Italy as a whole, is gay-friendly. Homosexuality is legal, and the age of consent is 16. Italians are generally more affectionate and physical than North Americans in all their friendships, and even straight men occasionally walk down the street with their arms around each other—however, kissing anywhere other than on the cheeks at greetings and goodbyes will draw attention. As you might expect, smaller towns tend to be less permissive than cities.

Italy's national associations and support networks for gays and lesbians are **ARCI-Gay and ArciLesbica.** The national websites are **www.arcigay.it** and **www.arcilesbica.it**, and most sizable cities have a local office. See **www.arcigay.it/comitati** for a searchable directory.

Mail & Postage   Sending a postcard or letter up to 20 grams, or a little less than an ounce, costs .95€ to other European countries, 2.30€ to North America, and a whopping 3€ to Australia and New Zealand. Full details on Italy's postal services are available at **www.poste.it** (some in English).

Mobile Phones   **GSM** (Global System for Mobile Communications) is a cellphone technology used by most of the world's countries that makes it possible to turn on a phone with a contract based in Australia, Ireland, the U.K., Pakistan, or almost every other corner of the world and have it work in Italy without missing a beat. (In the U.S., service providers like Sprint and Verizon use a different technology—CDMA—and phones on those networks won't work in Italy unless they also have GSM compatibility.)

Also, if you are coming from the U.S. or Canada, you may need a multiband phone. All travelers should activate "international roaming" on their account, so check with your home service provider before leaving.

But—and it's a *big* but—using roaming can be very expensive, especially if you access the Internet on your phone. It is usually much cheaper, once you arrive, to buy an Italian SIM card (the removable plastic card found in all GSM phones that is encoded with your phone number). This is not difficult, and is an especially good idea if you will be in Italy for more than a week. You can **buy a SIM card** at one of the many cellphone shops you will pass in every city. The main service providers are TIM, Vodafone, Wind, and 3 *(Tre)*. If you have an Italian SIM card in your phone, local calls may be as low as .10€ per minute, and incoming calls are free. Value prepaid data packages are available for each, as are micro- and nano-SIMs, as well as prepaid deals for iPads and other tablets. If you need 4G data speeds, you will pay a little more. Not every network allows **tethering**—be sure to ask if you need it. Deals on each network change regularly; for the latest see the website of one of this guide's authors: **www.donaldstrachan.com/dataroaming italy**. *Note:* Contract cellphones are often "locked" and will only work with a SIM card provided by the service provider back home, so check to see that you have an unlocked phone.

Buying a phone is another option, and you shouldn't have too much trouble finding one for about 30€. Use it, then recycle it or eBay it when you get home. It will save you a fortune versus alternatives such as roaming or using hotel room telephones.

Money & Costs   Frommer's lists exact prices in the local currency. The currency conversions quoted below were correct at press time. However, rates fluctuate, so before departing, consult a currency exchange website, such as **www.oanda.com/convert/ classic**, to check up-to-the-minute rates.

Like many European countries, Italy uses the euro as its currency. Euro coins are issued in denominations of .01€, .02€, .05€, .10€, .20€, and .50€, as well as 1€ and 2€; bills come in denominations of 5€, 10€, 20€, 50€, 100€, 200€, and 500€.

THE VALUE OF THE EURO VS. OTHER POPULAR CURRENCIES

€	Aus$	Can$	NZ$	UK£	US$
1	A$1.48	C$1.42	NZ$1.63	£0.70	$1.06

The evolution of international computerized banking and consolidated ATM networks has led to the triumph of plastic throughout the Italian peninsula—even if cold cash is still the most trusted currency in mom-and-pop joints. However, it is always a good idea to carry some cash, as small businesses may accept only cash or may claim that their credit card machine is broken to avoid paying fees to the card companies. Traveler's checks have gone the way of the Stegosaurus.

You'll get the best rate if you **exchange money** at a bank or one of its ATMs. The rates at "cambio/change/wechsel" exchange booths are invariably less favorable but still better than what you'd get exchanging money at a hotel or shop (a last-resort tactic only).

Visa and **MasterCard** are almost universally accepted. Some businesses also take **American Express,** especially at the higher end, but few take **Diners Club.**

Finally, be sure to let your bank know that you will be traveling abroad to avoid having your card blocked after a few days of big purchases far from home. *Note:* Many banks assess a 1% to 3% "transaction fee" on **all** charges you incur abroad (whether you're using the local currency or your native currency).

Police   For emergencies, call 🕐 **112** or 🕐 **113.** Italy has several different police forces, but there are only two you'll most likely ever need to deal with. The first is the *carabinieri* (**📞 112**), who normally only concern themselves with serious crimes, but point you in the right direction. The *polizia* (**📞 113**), whose city headquarters is called the *questura*, is the place to go for help with lost and stolen property or petty crimes.

Safety   Despite Sicily's reputation as a Mafia stronghold, the worst threats you'll likely face are the pickpockets who sometimes frequent touristy areas and public buses; keep your hands on your camera at all times and your valuables in an under-the-clothes money belt or inside zip-pocket. Don't leave anything valuable in a rental car overnight, and leave nothing visible in it at any time. If you are robbed, you can fill out paperwork at the nearest police station (*questura*), but this is mostly for insurance purposes or to get a new passport issued—don't expect them to spend any resources hunting down the perpetrator. In general, avoid public parks at night and dark city streets, especially in Palermo.

Senior Travel   Seniors and older people are treated with a great deal of respect and deference, but there are few specific programs, associations, or concessions made for them. British subjects can take advantage of senior discounts at museums, but Americans are usually not eligible.

Smoking   Smoking has been eradicated from inside restaurants, bars, and most hotels, so smokers tend to take outside tables at bars and restaurants. If you're keen for an alfresco table, you are essentially choosing a seat in the smoking section; requesting that your neighbor not smoke may not be politely received.

Student Travelers   An **International Student Identity Card (ISIC)** qualifies students for savings on rail passes, plane tickets, entrance fees, and more. The card is valid for 1 year. You can apply for the card online at **www.myisic.com** or in person at **STA Travel** (www.statravel.com; **📞 800/781-4040** in North America). If you're no longer a student but are still 26 and under, you can get an **International Youth Travel Card (IYTC)** and an **International Teacher Identity Card (ITIC)** from the same agency, either of which entitles you to some discounts. Students will also find that many university cities offer ample student discounts and inexpensive youth hostels.

Taxes   There's no sales tax added onto the price tag of purchases in Italy, but there is a 22% value-added tax (in Italy: IVA) automatically included in just about everything except basic foodstuffs like milk and bread. Entertainment, transport, hotels, and dining are among a group of goods taxed at a lower rate of 10%. For major purchases, you can get IVA refunded.

Tipping   In **hotels,** service is usually included in your bill. In family-run operations, additional tips are unnecessary and sometimes considered rude. In fancier places with a hired staff, however, you may want to leave a .50€ daily tip for the maid and pay the bellhop or porter 1€ per bag. In **restaurants,** a 1€ to 3€ per person "cover charge" is automatically added to the bill and in some tourist areas, especially Venice, another 10 to 15% is tacked on (except in the most unscrupulous of places, this will be noted on the menu somewhere; if unsure you should ask, è incluso il servizio?). It is not necessary to leave any extra money on the table, though it is not uncommon to leave up to 5€, especially for good service. Locals generally leave nothing. At **bars and cafes,** you can leave something very small on the counter for the barman (maybe 1€ if you have had several drinks), though it is not expected; there is no need to leave anything extra if you sit at a table, as they are likely already charging you double or triple the price you'd have paid standing at the bar. It is not necessary to tip **taxi** drivers, though it is common to round up the bill to the nearest euro or two.

Toilets   Public toilets are few and far between. Standard procedure is to enter a cafe, make sure the bathroom is not *fuori servizio* (out of order), and then order a cup of coffee before bolting to the facilities.

Index

PHOTO CREDITS